AF292409

SEX MAGIC

DIAGRAMS OF LOVE
ITHELL COLQUHOUN

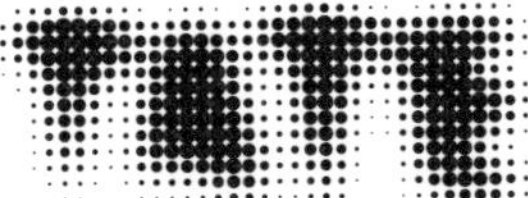

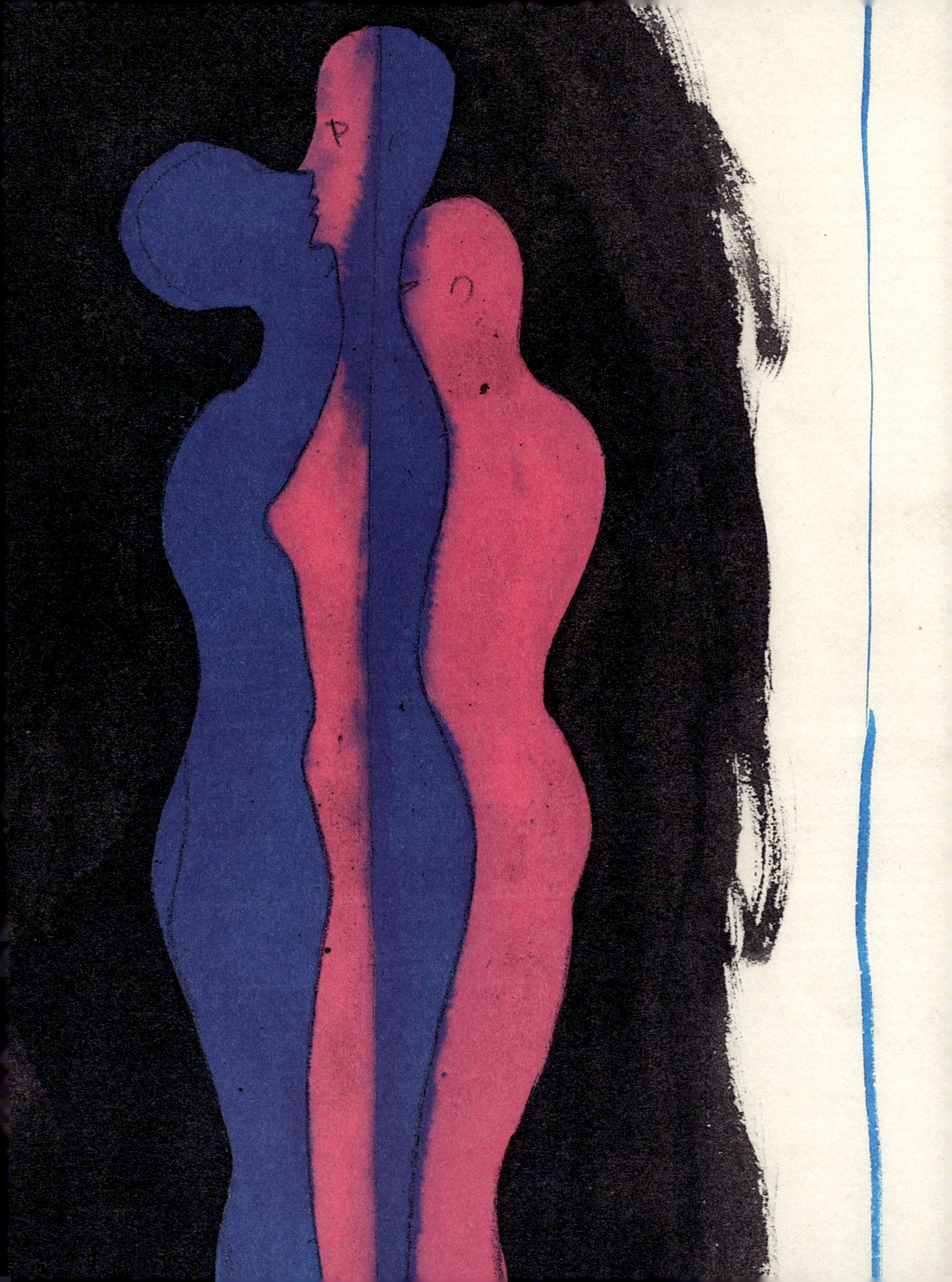

EXPLORING THE MAGICAL EROTIC CORPUS OF ITHELL COLQUHOUN

Amy Hale

From around 1939 to 1942, during the most intense and frightening years of the Second World War, Ithell Colquhoun created a body of obscure and explicit visual work focused on the principles of sacred sexual union. It is likely the earliest sustained and explicit visual expression of a sex magic programme associated with modern Western magical subcultures, and it was created by a woman. During these years, Colquhoun obsessively explored the world of alchemical erotica, producing sketches and watercolours of humans, angels and androgynous beings in various positions, couplings and threesomes, depicting transcendent ecstasies and apotheosis. This is the first time – maybe the only time – that we have an explicit, visually driven model of sex magic and esoteric sexuality that incorporates queer desires and even theorises multiple participants. Another groundbreaking feature of this corpus is subversion of the male gaze and the centring of women's sexual pleasure as a vehicle for connection with the divine. Although the collection was in essence private and practically undeveloped as a system, as a body of work it expands our understanding of the history of sex magic during the early twentieth century. It is nothing short of radical.

As of the time of writing, no clear or explicit documentation from the artist is known to exist that explains the rationale or symbolism of this body of work. In many ways, this is a true detective's journey, involving reading, decoding and educated guesswork – and there are still many questions left unanswered. What compelled Colquhoun to fixate on this topic? Was she hoping for a partner to help her complete the Great Work, the attainment of enlightenment, or was she working to come to peace with a realisation that union with the divine is primarily a solitary journey? Was she trying to engineer a programme of sex magic designed to be undertaken by occult adepts for the purpose of helping to heal a deeply wounded society? It would be lazy to conclude that she was simply driven by desire or obsessed by a lover, and this view would, frankly, reduce the radical implications of the project. Even Colquhoun's most personal magical explorations had universal and timeless applications, for she was a woman who always thought big. As historian of religions, Hugh Urban notes, regardless of how one conceives of sex magic, the one constant is that its aim is revolutionary.[1] For practitioners and promoters alike, sex magic is part of a wider programme of reform and revolution, and this is absolutely true of the work of Ithell Colquhoun.

About this collection

This book contains two conceptually related compilations. One collects the poems and images which Colquhoun labelled as *Diagrams of Love*, alongside a wider selection of alchemical erotic pieces and poetry which contain common esoteric themes and elements. Two poetic sequences named *Diagrams of Love* are held in Colquhoun's archives, each comprising small stanzas; they differ significantly, however, and Colquhoun scholar Richard Shillitoe has labelled these *Diagrams of Love I* and *II*, a convention we follow here. Both sequences are poems of love and longing. *Diagrams of Love I* – published in the literary magazine *The Glass* in 1953, but likely composed much earlier – more explicitly reflects themes of physical and emotional union and is more embodied, with references to sacred points on the body, physical connection, sensual knowledge and unfolding intimacy.

```
It is as though

We were both dead

Not lifeless, free

From conditions


Our coats of skin

Cast aside

We meet in a mother-naked

Flame
```

Diagrams of Love II feels more fragmented, and moves sharply from themes of a shared timeless spiritual bond to anticipation, doubt and fear of loss.

The small series of watercolours labelled *Diagrams of Love* poses interpretative challenges: they may or may not have been intended to accompany the poems. Some of these pieces appear to reflect themes in *Diagrams of Love I*, particularly those which reference sacred union, themes of circulation and blood, and the merging of fire and water. In these pieces we see references to the alchemical *Hieros Gamos* (see p.18 for more on this), esoteric Christianity, Rosicrucianism, sacrifice and possibly regeneration. There are also crudely executed lances piercing wounds that are somewhat vaginal, a metaphor that Colquhoun doesn't fully articulate, and eyes and lips which overlap in impossible ways. The degree to which Colquhoun considered these to be mature and complete works is generally unclear, although some, like *Heart of Corn*, which exists in several versions, were clearly intended to be shown and sold.

The pieces at the start of this book are connected with and are in many ways theoretical extensions of *Diagrams of Love*. These images fall into two broad categories: Colquhoun's experimental pieces referencing sex magic and esoteric sexuality, and erotica. It's evident that some of Colquhoun's visual musings on bodies were not just life studies but part of her own erotic responses: a beautiful erect penis, a tight focus on penetration, a naked reclining woman with nipples, lips, toenails and vulva delicately outlined in pink (pp.6, 9). This image and several others in this collection have similarities to Japanese *shunga*, or erotic art, images that were not only sexually explicit but, like those

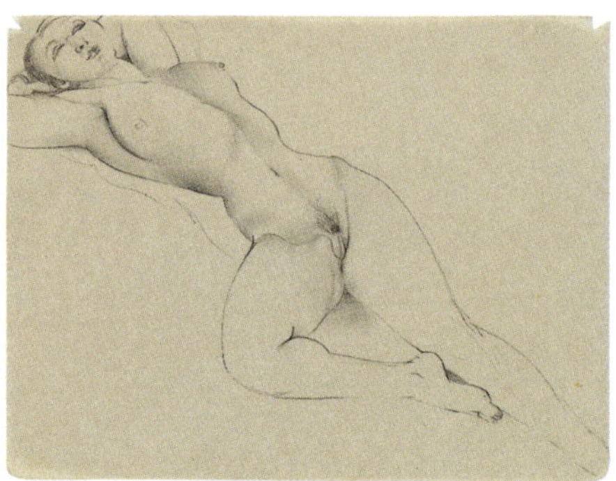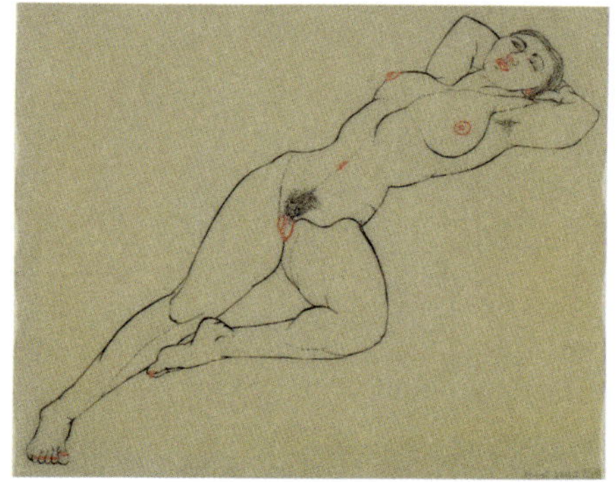

executed by Colquhoun, featured same-sex images and couplings in intricately challenging positions. *Shunga* was often created by woodblock, and the fact that Colquhoun also created a woodblock of one of her images of penetration not only reinforces the potential cultural influence, but may also suggest that she was planning to circulate these in some fashion. In fact, several of these pieces were clearly polished, signed and dated, although where she was going to display them remains a mystery.

Context of this body of work

1939 was the year that Colquhoun experienced the real peak of her public success and affiliation with the British surrealists, staging a joint show with Ronald Penrose at the Mayor Gallery and publishing pieces in the surrealist journal the *London Bulletin*. The same year, she visited Chemilieu in France with a cadre of surrealists, including Gordon Onslow Ford and Roberto Matta, to explore the theoretical outer reaches of automatism and extra dimensionality – a trip that altered her relationship with art, magic and the realms of the invisible. Yet in 1940, during the period in which she undertook this work, her relationship with the British surrealists reached a rather acrimonious end. Surrealist promoter and director of the London Gallery, Édouard Mesens, called a meeting to announce a list of rules and restrictions designed to secure the loyalty of the British surrealists and create ideological cohesion among them. Colquhoun elected to follow her own path explicitly rejecting the idea that she should put aside her esoteric interests or support political positions she likely didn't agree with.

Untitled sketches of two reclining nudes, one with pink accents
c.1941–2

Around this time Colquhoun began visiting Cornwall as an evacuee from London, and was exploring ideas about energy and sacred sites, developed in tandem to her erotic corpus. Like many artists of the time, Colquhoun was deeply emotionally affected by the Second World War, and it is possible that the idealism and redemption of humanity, suggested by the promise of esoteric sexuality, was a way for her to envision a new way of being. Perhaps she believed that society could overcome its divisions through an integration with the sacred, fuelled by energy from the portals of sacred landscapes and individuals' elevated connections with one another, as they embraced the potential to access dimensions more peaceful and enlightened than the unstable world around them.

Women and the history of sex magic

Colquhoun's work is part of a wider conversation about sacred sexuality in 'the West' (itself a deeply problematic construct), how it should be accomplished and what its aims should be. As with so many issues, once we focus on women's contributions, the entire nature of the conversation changes. As a result, our historical understanding of what sex magic is and how it should best be performed is really quite restricted: even in the systems that stress the importance of women's pleasure, sex magic is generally characterised and defined by the male sexual experience. Most contemporary sex magic curricula assume that the magus is male, while women are often conceptualised as passive and receptive in the sexual act. Although many occultists are now retheorising sex magic for women, trans and non-binary people, there is no argument that most of the historical sources championed today were primarily designed by and for men. Similarly, sex magic is historically also typified by heterosexual dynamics, essentialising and normalising social roles and expectations of men and women through the defining and limiting language of science, most typically that of electrical polarity; male homosexual sex magic, which has rarely been historically addressed outside of the work of Aleister Crowley, has been vilified as abhorrent at worst and ineffective at best due to an inability to 'complete a circuit' with both gender 'polarities',[2] while women's homoerotic sex magic is, for all intents and purposes, invisible.

Although women have continually been involved in theorising sex magic and esoteric sexuality since the late nineteenth century, most scholars (and certainly many occultists) have downplayed or ignored their contributions. Hugh Urban's exploration of modern sex magic defines it as having a focus on optimising orgasm for either material or transcendent ends.[3] This makes a certain sense when examining a specific subset of the literature, but women's esoteric sexuality or even sex magic does not always have the same orgasmic focus or end result. If anyone is familiar with modern sex magic at all, they tend to equate it with the career of the infamous Crowley, who believed sexuality was a liberatory force, and who conducted sex magic 'operations' with specialised partners, known as his 'Scarlet Women', male lovers and prostitutes throughout his life.

Yet the man most responsible for initially promoting sex magic and sacred sexuality among modern occult circles was Paschal Beverly Randolph, an African American spiritualist and Rosicrucian whose radical view of the relationship between sexuality and enlightenment laid the groundwork for the modern esoteric language of sex magic. His 1874 book *Eulis!* is a combination of marriage advice, social reform manifesto and rambling esoteric treatise. Although Randolph didn't exactly promote the equality of the sexes, he did believe that the Divine was dual sexed and that each gender was incomplete without the other.

Often, women's esoteric sexuality was designed to socially reposition women and to help gain some control of reproduction, but it also had a focus on pleasure and cultivating women's orgasms as a way of improving marital (and thus wider social) relations. These reforming efforts, combined with the scientific and spiritual language around magnetism and energy exchange, were at the heart of women's early engagements with esoteric sexuality in the nineteenth and early twentieth century, some of which may have influenced Colquhoun's images and preoccupations.

As might be expected, the women of this period who theorised about sacred sexuality and its social implications had a different perspective from their male counterparts about what should be emphasised in the practice. Early sex theorists in general, including Randolph, were concerned with the mistreatment of women, spousal rape and the effects of unwanted pregnancies on women's lives. Alice Bunker Stockham was a Chicago-based gynaecologist, women's dress reform advocate and vegetarian, who promoted both birth control and the role of women's sexual pleasure in strengthening marriages. Her influential 1896 book *Karezza* advocated restrictions on male ejaculation – as found in both Indian Tantra and the New York-based Oneida Community active in the nineteenth century – to reduce

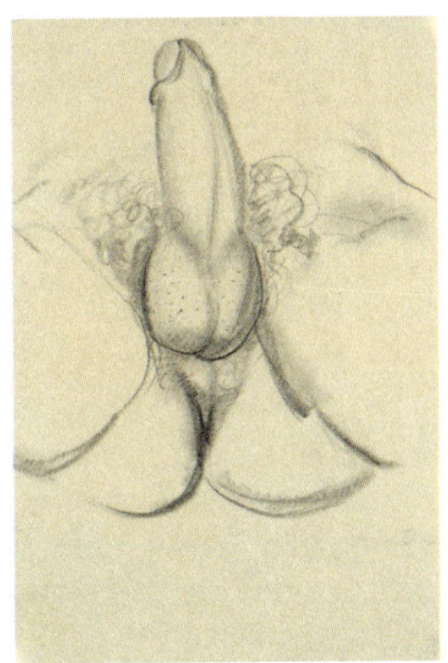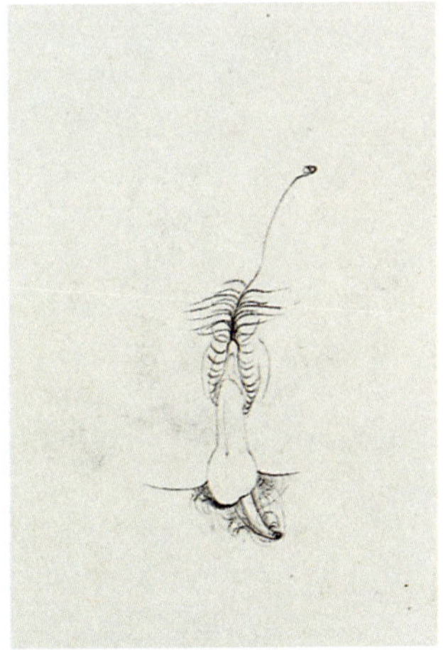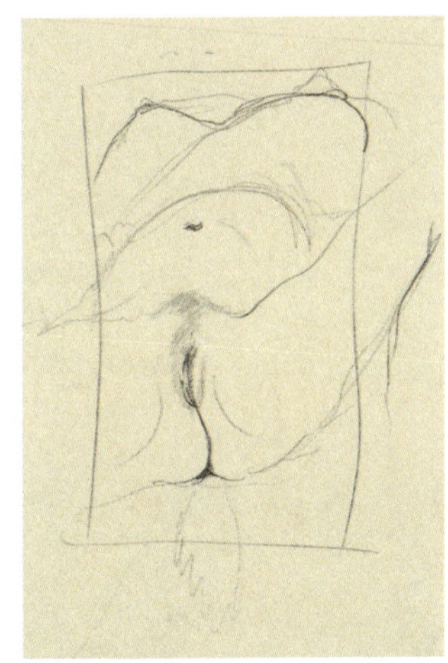

pregnancies and enhance women's sexual pleasure. The American feminist activist Ida Craddock was likely the most noteworthy of the early women writers about esoteric sexuality, advocating for women to be able to choose when to have sex and when to conceive. Her remarkable book *Heavenly Bridegrooms* (1918) explored a mythical history of women taking spirit husbands, and also chronicled her own experience with her spirit husband from another dimension, with whom she apparently had incredible sex. Colquhoun may have seen Aleister Crowley's 1919 review of *Heavenly Bridegrooms* in *The Blue Equinox*; she occasionally drew on Craddock's themes of an initiatory tradition of virginal priestesses, such as Mary, and their conceptions resulting from intercourse with spirit husbands.

Yet these early women advocates of a conscious and sacred sexuality were likely more concerned with reaping concrete social benefits than with promoting an esoteric path to divine union for women. Even in the idiosyncratic sex magic performed by Russian occultist Maria De Naglowska's Parisian order, the Brotherhood of the Golden Arrow in the early 1930s, women were passive: it was their purity which was transformative, not their desire for self-actualisation. If the goal of sex magic was seen to be transformative – to make one into a deity on earth – that seemed an avenue available only to men.

Yet union with deity seemed to be Colquhoun's explicit goal, and her esoteric explorations, despite their oddly empirical character, were hardly demure. In this collection, the expectations for women's visual erotic culture are blown apart. Colquhoun often focuses the

Untitled sketches of genitals and intercourse, c.1940–2
Graphite on paper

lens tightly on disembodied body parts and genitals and the moment of penetration, depicted in the incredible detail that might be more expected from a pornography publication aimed at men. One pencil sketch immediately recalls Gustave Courbet's 1866 *The Origin of the World* (p.9), likely reimagined through Sapphic eyes, but which for Colquhoun may have also been the basis of a landscape, an inspiration famously employed in *Tree Anatomy* 1942 where Colquhoun fashions a hole in a tree as a barely disguised explicit and rather cavernous vulva.

A unique feature of this collection is Colquhoun's explicit interest in mutuality and women's sexual pleasure as a key to apotheosis. Randolph, Stockham and Craddock all framed women's pleasure as an important way of demonstrating the 'magnetism' between a married and functional couple, strengthening not only the marriage, but also society as a whole. For some sex magicians, however, women's bodies were seen as a tool. Crowley was notorious for working sex magical operations with prostitutes who were not told (and therefore certainly not consenting) about their role in a magical working. The Italian esotericist Julius Evola believed that women were simply unable to experience spiritual transcendence and must therefore be the medium for men's development.[4] Perhaps the coldest assessment of women's role in sex magic comes from De Naglowska, who believed that women's purity provided the fulcrum for the spiritual evolution of men. Women should not experience sexual pleasure, which was reserved for men; instead, women must remain passive, satisfied with inner transformations, not physical or carnal satisfaction, helping to create the Perfect Man through an ethics of service.[5] It is sad indeed that De Naglowska likely aptly characterised the genuine social expectations for so many women, who were implicitly or explicitly told to repress their desires and aspirations for the good of everyone else.

Yet, nowhere in Colquhoun's life did she sign up for that programme. Women's sexual and spiritual subjectivity is the focus of many of these pieces, and the importance of mutual pleasure sees couples adopting awkward and complicated sexual positions (p.38). There are also a number of images showing women receiving oral sex – though interestingly never showing it performed on men (pp.42-3). While spermatophagy and the consuming of mixed male and female sexual fluids is another key theme in modern sex magic, this practice seems to have no apparent role in Colquhoun's works.[6] In the most developed image of the magical sequence, it would appear that the woman who has been penetrated has become a non-gendered being, achieving transformation as a result of this divine union.

The 'science' of sex magic

Much of Colquhoun's erotic body of work, and indeed many of her visual magical experiments, can be understood within the emerging discourses of science and technology in the first part of the twentieth century, when the boundaries between science and magic were permeable. Although Colquhoun was concerned with notions of spiritual enlightenment that today seem wildly subjective, twentieth-century magical culture was inherently entwined with ideas about empiricism, science and progress. Sex magic – much like magic itself – is often defined by ideas of repeatable techniques and predictability.

Most, but not all, sex magic in the Western tradition relies on the language of nineteenth-century science regarding the revealing of things previously unseen: electromagnetic radiation, atomic theory, evolution and theories of other hidden dimensions. Theosophy's language around the 'occult sciences' was influential in reinforcing ideas about the relationship between occult practice and emerging methods of observation and testing, mingled with the rhetoric of the continuity of an ancient wisdom tradition.[7] Central to emerging theories of sex magic were the newer scientised discourses around 'energy', which developed from eighteenth-century theories of magnetism and vitalism and incorporated a number of traditional esoteric concepts bridging both East and West, including notions of a vital life force, Indian concepts of prana and Chinese theories of qi. As the science of the unseen developed, 'energy' and 'electromagnetism' became the frameworks that positioned esoteric vital forces within scientific discourses. Yet the language and aesthetics of sex magic blends the ancient and modern, suggesting mythic origins in the spiritual technologies of lost worlds such as Atlantis or the practices of Indian Tantra – wisdom which is always in the process of being recovered or revealed to those who are ready to receive it.

A typical description of the principles underlying sex magic as characterised by Dion Fortune or Randolph would explain that essentialised masculine and feminine 'currents' combine through sacred sexual techniques of energy-raising to create a circuit that could be used to propel states of enlightenment and bliss, or potentially to even power more mundane and worldly achievements.

Randolph's writings provide much of the vocabulary and foundational principles of sex magic that have been transmitted in contemporary occult culture; these certainly laid the groundwork for Colquhoun's own explorations. Here, Randolph characterises

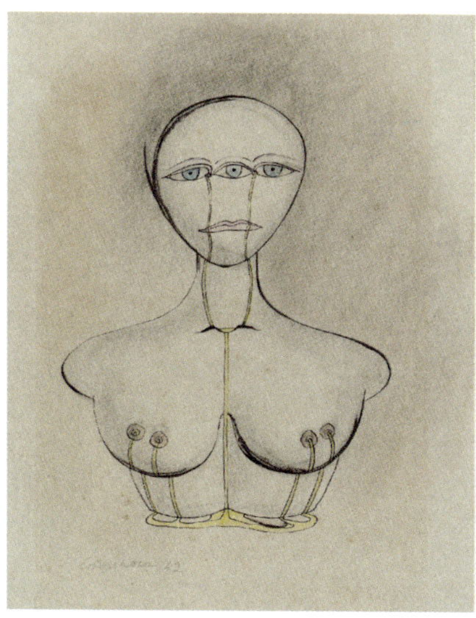

sacred sex using the esoterically tinged scientific language of his day, describing the electric currents that inhabit bodies and that move between them during sexual intercourse:

> Let me restate the law in clearer terms: 1st. The joys of Love are consequent upon the rush of nervous fluid along the nerval fibrils, filamental cords, or wires of the system, centring in the vital ganglia of either sex. When it flows alone it is electric. When it contacts on both sides it is magnetic. 2nd. The fulness of Love-joy depends upon the plethora of vital life and nerve-aura stored up in the ganglia of the system, but especially upon the greater or less stock magazined within the mystic cripts [sic] appointed of Nature for that purpose.[8]

Fortune employs similar metaphors in *The Esoteric Philosophy of Love and Marriage* (1924), which likely contributed to the theoretical underpinnings of Colquhoun's project. Inspired by the Theosophical sevenfold schema of the evolution of bodies and consciousness, Fortune lays out what she sees as the appropriate conditions under which people can employ sexual union as the ultimate way of gaining enlightenment. Great emphasis is placed on the suitability of the participants in sex magic, and Colquhoun's schema appears to reinforce the idea that the participants need to be spiritually

Untitled (Three-eyed figure) 1942
Watercolour and ink on paper
47 × 38.3

advanced. Unlike Crowley, Fortune stresses that sacred sex is not for earthly gain or for spell work, but is instead the merging of two advanced beings uniting their astral bodies to create a single etheric entity. She provides a detailed discussion of gender and polarity, describing esoteric sexuality in terms of electric currents, with each participant essentially a negative or positive pole on a battery. However, her take on gender and polarity allows for a bit of wiggle room, which may have appealed to Colquhoun: although Fortune describes the male force as active and the female force as passive, she explains that on the astral plane these polarities are reversed.

Many of the pieces in the *Diagrams of Love* series and in Colquhoun's other erotic works are concerned with openings on the body that can serve as portals where energy can be received – either from the electromagnetic currents under the earth or a divine source – or exchanged. It is evident from her art and writings that Colquhoun based her own theories partially on Indian esoteric ideas about the flow of life force, or prana: she refers to nadis and chakras, points where energy flows or is concentrated in both the physical body and in the astral body. In *Second Adam* (p.63) we see a luminous naked figure, possibly representing a hermaphroditic Christ, radiating with energy and containing alchemical vessels in his interior cavity. *Snow Maiden* 1940 shows a figure with what might be interpreted as rainbow centres of energy at various points in the body. Colquhoun believed that both bodies and sacred landscapes had the ability to generate and transmit forces and that these connections could be transformative. In *The Sunset Birth* c.1942, for example, we see energy streams resembling nadis running through the etheric form of a woman engaging with the Men-an-Tol, an ancient stone site in Cornwall. Colquhoun's painting of c.1940 *The Thirteen Streams of Magnificent Oil* draws on British occultist MacGregor Mathers's *Kabbalah Unveiled* to demonstrate the openings of the body through which the divine might enter; flowing down from the beard of Macroprosopus, said to illuminate all things which are inferior. Colquhoun expands on this in an essay, 'Openings of the Body', published in 1970 but reflecting a much earlier engagement with the topic, in which she theorises that the Theosophical concept of openings or energy gates in the body may allow for the transfer of divine energy. As women have one more opening than men, this indicates that women are 'more highly evolved and more specialized'.[9]

It would seem that Colquhoun was suggesting that people could exchange energy through various channels and in various positions in a sort of sexual yoga, with the aim of liberation and transcendence through divine union. Sketches in this series show a couple facing each other in a Tantric *yab-yum*, also known as the lotus embrace, an upright position likely meant to facilitate energy exchange between the bodies (p.31). Also evident in some of these works are visual streams of energy, probably indicating Kundalini and other flows of energy throughout the body that would be occurring during sexual union. Some of the figures appear to incorporate some form of sacred geometry: one contorted couple is clearly attempting to fit their bodies into a hexagram (p.29); another may be trying to wind their way into a cosmic lemniscate. In some pieces, the entry points for these energies are indicated by red dots where the bodies need to be in some way touching, such as at the nipples (pp.56–7).

The coordination of these energy flows into a single, unified stream is one important visual motif for Colquhoun in these pieces. She works through various levels of abstraction, starting with the couple in union in a hexagram, the central column of their bodies aligned. In subsequent drawings, Colquhoun removes the limbs and other details, but we can still see the penetration, the spinal column, and the energy flow. In some images the body's central column almost resembles lips. In the most elaborated form of this process, *The Bird or the Egg* (p.75), we see the culmination of the union of the phallus and the grail, with the transformed birdlike androgyne emerging from the central stream of energy, a crown of energy streaming upward from the top of the head demonstrating connection with the undifferentiated divine source. What started as a depiction of a ritualised sacred sex act transforms, through repeated iterations, into the representation of the magical outcome of the physical process.

Esoteric influences

Without any written documentation from the artist on this corpus, discerning Colquhoun's vision involves following threads in her writings, theorising about her imagery and investigating a variety of esoteric writings to form an understanding about her project. Colquhoun had a diverse set of occult influences for this project, including Kabbalah, tantra, alchemy and Golden Dawn ritual. Most likely, Colquhoun's initial inspiration came from her cousin Edward Garstin's alchemical text, *The Secret Fire: An Alchemical Study* (1932), which was primarily an exposition on the nature and symbolism of spiritual fire, or life force, the vehicle bridging the divide between the human and the divine. Colquhoun was also likely familiar with

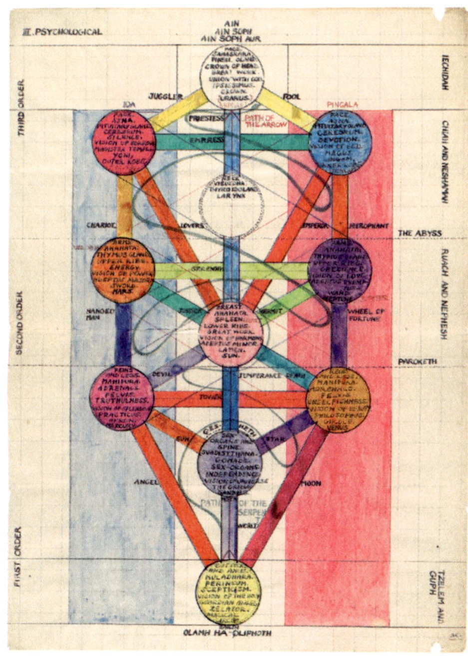

Kabbalistic Tree of Life diagram: III Psychological
date not known
Ink and gouache on
paper, 76 x 56

the general corpus of writings about sex magic in circulation among occultists in the early twentieth century, including early Ordo Templi Orientis[10] writers both pre- and post-Crowley. Having been born in Northern India, Colquhoun also took a keen interest in Tantra for parts of her life. Like Garstin, Colquhoun was certainly also familiar with the works of John Woodroffe, whose works (written as Arthur Avalon) helped to bring a radical set of practices and ideas to English speaking audiences. Colquhoun's interests would have resonated with ideas of non-duality and the importance of the female Shakti as the source of divine power. It is also exceptionally likely that Colquhoun had access to Richard Burton's edition of the iconic sex manual, the *Kama Sutra*, first published in 1883, with its wide-ranging and diverse descriptions of human sexual and erotic behaviours.

The influence of W.B. Yeats on Colquhoun's various magical and artistic projects can also not be underestimated. Often marked by alchemical, esoteric and Tantric themes interwoven with Irish nationalism and romantic Celticism, Yeats's work in many ways provides a template for Colquhoun's pursuits throughout her life. Colquhoun considered Yeats a prophet, and she was especially interested in the challenging revelatory text channelled with his wife Georgie, *A Vision*. Published in 1925 and revised in 1937, *A Vision* included wide-ranging philosophies about the nature of humanity, time and history. It is very likely that Colquhoun's interest in sex magic as an engine of social transformation was inspired by her close readings of this text. But is it at all possible that the work of Yeats and his explicit focus on sexuality at the end of his life prompted this project of Colquhoun's? While it is conjecture, it is possible: Colquhoun appears to have met Yeats in 1937 and Yeats died in January of 1939, the year that Colquhoun began her project in earnest. Might the sexual preoccupations of Yeats's later years have planted a metaphorical seed inspiring this project?

Colquhoun makes explicit allusions to this project in two writings: the poem 'Union Pacific' and her short essay 'The Water Stone of the Wise', both highly indebted to Yeats. 'The Water Stone of the Wise' was published in *New Road* in 1943, in the early years of her marriage with Toni Del Renzio, as a response to André Breton's 1942 'Prolegomena to A Third Surrealist Manifesto (Or Not)' in which he suggests the power of creating new myths to inspire social change.[11] Colquhoun offers up an alchemically driven myth of social redemption, inspired by Yeats's notion of the 'solved antimony', the cosmic perfection derived from sexual union, the merging of opposites. The title comes from the 1619 alchemical treatise, *The Sophic Hydrolith*, which reveals that the Philosopher's Stone is the earthly substance of Christ, or the perfect Light of God. For Colquhoun, the Philosopher's Stone, the Light of God, is accessed through the hermaphroditic state deriving from the union of opposites that will create the societal conditions for the cessation of oppression:

> No more tyrants and victims, no more the fevered alternations of that demon star which sponsored the births of de Sade and von Sacher-Masoch – but the hermaphrodite whole, opposites bound together in mitigating embrace by a silkworm's thread … The new myth, the myth of the Siamese Twins, will make of [Oedipus] a forgotten bogey.

> In one of the planets' airy houses live the Twins, a boy and a girl, perpetually joined by an ectoplasmic substance which is warmed by the solar and lunar currents of their bodies. They cannot part, nor do anything apart. They eat and breathe each other day and night.

They are united face to face, having passed forward to the
condition of the androgynous egg. Their faculty is dream, their
body-of-fate the stream of images – sensual transpositions –
induced by the incandescence of their own body and mind.
They have no privacy from each other, and desire none, since
theirs is a unity conscious of its own elements. They weigh down
equally each scale of the Balance, and as the two Fishes, are held
together in watery dance by a single cord.[12]

The poem 'Union Pacific' (see p.44) is clearly a response to Yeats's
'Ribb Denounces Patrick', a section from his 1934 collection
Supernatural Songs.[13] Colquhoun's poem, which uses the same metre
and even employs phrases from Yeats's work, could uncharitably be
characterised as derivative, but it is more likely that she is responding
in kind to his ideas. Like Yeats, she is speculating on divinity, and
more specifically, how the Gods may find themselves taking human
or incarnate form. Here Colquhoun also provides clues about the
colour scheme she uses in her work, the fusing of scarlet and cerulean
suggesting the unity of bodies, of souls and of course also the
integration of self.

What seems certain is that the goal of Colquhoun's project was the
formation of the Divine Androgyne, and the individual and collective
transcendence of gender – an important theme of the esoteric
landscape of the early twentieth century.[14] The Hermaphrodite
or Divine Androgyne had been a significant focus, certainly, of
Renaissance alchemy and Rosicrucianism, and some occult readings
of the Kabbalah. It infused the work of the symbolist Joséphin Peladán,
Martinism, and even the Hermetic Order of the Golden Dawn. Broadly
speaking, as one version of this esoteric story goes, it was believed
that humans before the Fall were genderless, perfected beings and
that the refinement of the soul – which was for many the aim of occult
practice – would result in this state of androgyny. For Colquhoun this
principle would have been reinforced by the alchemical collections
she loved and the Neoplatonic writings of people such as George
Robert Stow Mead, founder of the esoteric Quest Society, to which
Colquhoun belonged while studying at the Slade from the late 1920s
to the early 1930s. Another primary inspiration for her interest in
the Divine Androgyne was likely Samuel 'MacGregor' Mathers's
1887 translation of sections of Christian Knorr von Rosenroth's
seventeenth-century text *Kabbala Denudata* as *The Kabbalah Unveiled*.
Several chapters comment on the importance of the unification of

the male and female to achieve wholeness and spiritual completion, replicating the conjoined souls of Adam and Eve prior to the Fall:

> When the Male is joined with the Female, They both constitute one complete body, and all the Universe is in a state of happiness, because all things receive blessing from Their perfect body. And this is an Arcanum.
>
> And hence that which is not both Male and Female together is called half a body. Now, no blessing can rest upon a mutilated and defective being, but only upon a perfect place and upon a perfect being, and not at all in an incomplete being.
>
> And a semi-complete being cannot live forever, neither can it receive blessing for ever.[15]

This is a clear directive calling for a gendered balance in the universe, and Colquhoun took it as such, finding further resonance in the alchemical symbolism of the *Hieros Gamos*. This is the sacred marriage of the King and Queen (sometimes brother and sister), represented in the stage of *conjunction* resulting in the Divine Androgyne, the union of spirit and matter, the Great Work. In these arcane texts Colquhoun found affirmation that the divine feminine and the role of women had not been erased from the Western mysteries: women were critical to spiritual attainment, individually and socially, and without widespread cultural acknowledgement of the divine feminine, there would be no paradise on earth.

It appears that Colquhoun's ideas about the transition to the androgynous state took a number of different forms. In many of these images, the gender of one of the partners is unclear. In one case it would appear that a woman is, during the process of this sacred union, moving from a gendered to an ungendered state. These works include images of bodies that for Colquhoun would have been coded as 'male' and 'female', sometimes indicated by a penis, vulva or rounder breasts. Yet, there are many points where a person visually marked as female (longer hair, feminised face, breasts, possibly Colquhoun herself) is sexually engaged with a figure whose nature and gender is very unclear indeed: often they are bald with sexual organs consistently obscured. In fact, this treatment is so consistent it can hardly be accidental. Is this an evolved human, an angel, or perhaps

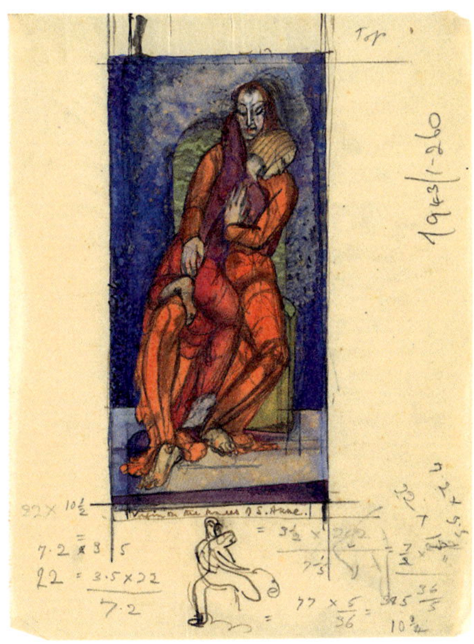

*Untitled study for Virgin
on the Knees of St.Anne*
c.1940–3
Watercolour and
ink on paper

a spirit lover? Additionally, some of the images include three people,
most often two images coded as 'masculine' and one as 'feminine'
– although, again, the sex of the blue or indigo figures is not always
certain in these pieces. It is possible that the other partner could be
an astral entity or even represent the Holy Guardian Angel, thought
of in some occult traditions as a unique force which guides the
higher aspirations of self. Perhaps Colquhoun believed that engaging
with your anima or animus would serve just as well as having an
earthly partner.

Some of these images are clearly homoerotic, which suggests that
the intended outcome can be achieved without the opposite currents
being embedded into physical sexes: only the energetic currents need
to be polarised, not the bodies themselves. The sketch *The Virgin on
the Knees of St. Anne* – in which we see the Tantric transmission of an
esoteric current from mother to daughter as Mary, clad in the blue
and red of divine attainment, receives the energetic current from
her mother, dressed in orange Buddhist robes – might, in fact, be an
imagining of Colquhoun in the arms of her lover of a decade earlier,
Kyria Kazou. The idea of same sex, particularly lesbian, energetic
transmission would have been quite a radical suggestion in the

occult circles of the early 1940s, as homosexual magic was certainly considered deviant by writers such as Dion Fortune.

Colquhoun's own relationship to same sex attraction was plausibly a point of difficulty for her, and this body of work shows that she was most likely trying to make sense of it through the figure of the androgyne. Colquhoun had experienced sexual and romantic attractions to women, making it logical that she would theorise about lesbian energetics. Later in life, however, she appeared to reject the lesbian union as a way to secure ultimate attainment. In an undated essay written after the breakup of her marriage, probably in the mid-1950s, Colquhoun relates the difficulties that intelligent, spiritually advanced women have in finding romantic and sexual partners, observing that in general there will be fewer suitable male partners for such women. She notes, with sympathy, that women of attainment may reasonably find themselves interested in a lesbian relationship, but that this will ultimately stifle the woman's potential for achievement: 'It is understandable if a woman so placed is tempted to back into some kind of lesbian relationship, but if she does so it will be to an adolescent phase and will tend to vitiate what she has achieved.'[16] One suspects that her struggle around same sex attraction in a heteronormative society was never fully reconciled.

Colquhoun's erotic corpus also visually reflects esoteric ideas about 'The Christ' as a perfected and genderless human, promoted in the late nineteenth century by Christian Theosophists, Anna Kingsford and Edward Maitland but also echoed in the rituals of the Hermetic Order of the Golden Dawn and seen in the esoteric Christian occult society, the Cromlech Temple, with which Colquhoun evidently was familiar. The positioning of many of the pieces in this collection is clearly in a cruciform shape, with figures oriented with arms out. In some cases, as in *Diagrams of Love* 1941[17] (p.89), we see a small red figure appearing to be crucified within a blue Earth mother-type figure. It is useful to understand the complexity of what Christ meant in the esoteric context of the groups that were inspiring Colquhoun's work. 'The Christ', or the 'Philosopher's Stone', was a state to be attained that signified union with the divine – a state which transcended history, culture and religion. Christ, like Adam before the Fall, was sometimes believed to also have been androgynous, and it is this state of perfected, divinely infused humanity that Colquhoun was trying to achieve through sexual union: the exchange of energy from the divine source, through the bodies, and back again.

Colquhoun's corpus also engages with a series of enigmatic

themes relating to sacrifice and regeneration, referencing the esoteric Christianity, sacrificial Gods and Grail symbolism that had been working their way into early Hermetic sex magic symbolism since the very early writings of the Ordo Templi Orientis. Like many ritualists of her time, Colquhoun was also interested in the Grail legend as emblematic of a uniquely European (and for many, specifically British) coded tale of sacred kingship and fertility, and this theme appears in her paintings and essays periodically throughout her life. Wagner's *Parsifal* (1882), like other variants of the Arthurian corpus in the late nineteenth and early twentieth century, was believed to have actually contained esoteric teachings and even the foundations for fertility rituals, which inspired the sex magic commentaries of the Ordo Templi Orientis's Theodor Reuss in 1914, later elaborated on in Charles Stanfield Jones's 1923, *Chalice of Ecstasy*.[18] Jessie Weston's 1920 bestseller, *From Ritual to Romance* also theorised that Arthurian legend arose from a native British esoteric system of fertility rites in which the lance and the grail were key metaphors for the phallus and the vagina, the lingam and the yoni.[19]

In *Diagrams of Love* and in her wider artistic corpus, Colquhoun symbolically layers figures and concepts which reference The Christ and The Fisher King as lovers seeking divine union. The sacrifice of the Arthurian Fisher King becomes James Frazier's sacrificial king of the dying wheat and harvest, who can also be equated with the Christ figure and the ancient Egyptian Osiris. In her writings, as in her images, Colquhoun incorporates cruciform images, piercings, wounds, hearts and blood. The lance in the wound becomes an erotic metaphor for both sacrifice and completion. The grail, however, is restorative: in the one image of Colquhoun's where the grail is explicit, *The Bird or The Egg* (p.75), it is from the union of phallus and grail that the hermaphrodite whole emerges.

Colour and form

Colquhoun was exceptionally interested in the power of colour and compact imagery to penetrate the subconscious. She was taken by alchemical emblems and esoteric heraldry and referred to them often in her surrealist writings. Her earlier esoteric art from her student years recalled tarot cards (and in fact she occasionally used tarot imagery), alchemical art and Renaissance iconography. Yet in her magical experiments from the 1930s onward she moves from the emblem to the diagram, with its accompanying scientific context, bearing a different sort of visual authority. From the early nineteenth century onward, the diagram bridges subjective esotericism with the language of empiricism,

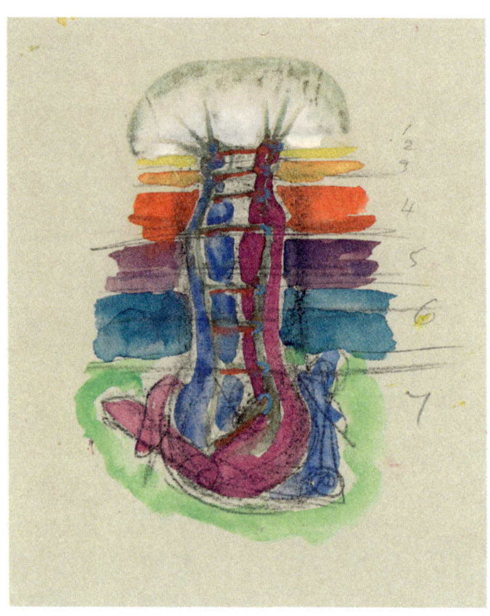

becoming an aspect of the visual expression of the scientism of modern occultism.[20] In many ways this is a form of abstraction meant to capture or represent a thing which is utterly unrepresentable, wrapping it in the language of empiricism. In fact, the diagrammatic tendency blurs the awkward boundaries between abstraction and representation that underpin so much of modern esoteric art. The impact of the diagram is seen in the thought-forms of Theosophists C.W. Leadbeater and Annie Besant, and in the abstracted work of Hilma af Klint and Olga Fröbe-Kapteyn. It's also seen in the impenetrable gyres and cones of Yeats's *A Vision*, so influential to Colquhoun's thought, as well as in Tantric schematics and the diagrams of the Hermetic Order of the Golden Dawn that form the key visual and theoretical foundations for many of her magical images.

Although the work in this series is not wholly abstract, these pieces can be interpreted as schematics, as they are tightly focused and without any real background or visual context. Some may function as abstractions of key concepts, perhaps similar to Theosophical thought-forms. Even the title *Diagrams of Love* recalls Benjamin Betts's 1887 project to create mathematical representations of human emotions such as love and the experience of beauty. Louisa Cook, in her interpretation and analysis of Betts's work, discusses energy and polarity as key terms describing consciousness – showing the degree

Untitled sketch of conjoined couple under a rainbow
c.1940–2
Watercolour and graphite on paper

22

to which these ideas had permeated the overlapping ideas about science and the spirit.[21]

Can we think of Colquhoun's images as erotic 'Diagrams', expressions of both desire and process? Many of her magical experiments, and some finished artworks, take the initial form of a diagram, frequently drafted on graph paper. For Colquhoun the universe was rulebound, and she was interested in honing techniques. Her diagrams, and especially these erotic works, do not speak to passion, although they do in some cases centralise and indeed operationalise pleasure. These works indicate the development of a method and its potential outcomes, and colour and form are key to decoding them.

The colour theory of the Golden Dawn was a primary influence on Colquhoun's work in general, and her palette for this series appears to have been drawn predominantly from the Kabbalistic King Scale used by the Golden Dawn, which centres around the colours of the spectrum of visible light. The King Scale for the Sephiroth and paths of the tree is also found on the colour wheel at the centre of the Golden Dawn Rose Cross. The centrality of colour theory to the teachings of the Golden Dawn is likely one of the reasons Colquhoun, as an artist, gravitated to the Order. A knowledge lecture within the Golden Dawn Adeptus Minor ritual called the Book of the Path of The Chameleon, outlines the colour theory used in generating the colours of the Tree of Life. The Golden Dawn employs the metaphor of 'seeking the light' throughout its teachings, and the rainbow is light broken down into discernible colours. Understanding colour not merely as symbol but as force and entity itself was an important part of Colquhoun's magical and artistic projects.

Colquhoun's visual construction of this series was remarkably consistent. Male figures are a brilliant blue and females are violet-red or magenta, colours that respectively represent the male sphere of Chokmah and the female sphere of Binah in the King Scale of the Kabbalistic Tree of Life.[22] These colours descend from the top Sephiroth, Kether, which for Colquhoun symbolises union with deity, perfect love and the ultimate transcendence of gender. We see an early iteration of this colour scheme in her 1933 *Song of Songs* (p.25), where a magenta and blue banner curls over a woman who embraces a quite androgynous lover:

He brought me to the banqueting house, and his banner over me was love.

23

Notably, in her poem 'Union Pacific', Colquhoun specifically refers to the colours 'scarlet' and 'cerulean' as representative of the two polarities which will mingle and ultimately be transcended for the perfected union. Scarlet and cerulean blue are specifically named in Exodus 28:4 and 28:16 as two of the colours which will be used in constructing the priestly garment, the ephod, and its breastplate.[23]

The other colour combinations Colquhoun employs in this series are harder to decode, but likely have to do with other combinations on parts of the spectrum. Rainbows also appear in Colquhoun's wider corpus and also occasionally in this body of work, suggesting that she may have been building a programme of sex magic suitable specifically for the Golden Dawn adept. One sketch, clearly meant as a colour key, features a central abstraction of a stick figure couple in a *yab–yum* pose in blue and magenta (p.31). Flanking this primary figure is a further series of stick figures in different opposing colours on the spectrum, representing different, possibly Kabbalistic, colour schematics. Occasionally Colquhoun worked with figures in combinations of green and yellow; or red, yellow, and orange; or pink and indigo. Interestingly, a number of these figures are clearly ungendered.

It seems likely that Colquhoun was experimenting with the idea of creating a sex magic system designed for the Western magician, inspired by Tantric technologies but replete with symbolism drawn from 'Western' sources, including the Golden Dawn, the Cromlech Temple and the early Ordo Templi Orientis. Maybe she saw a gap and was trying to fill it. However, much of this project was either abandoned or incorporated into her work in more subtle ways. Her idiosyncratic history of the Golden Dawn, *The Sword of Wisdom* (1975) included an appendix dedicated to Tantra and speculations about Golden Dawn sexual practices, yet the theoretical material suggested in this collection is not hinted at or elaborated on in that essay. Although some of the colour coding in this project would reappear in her work for years to come, and she continued to produce erotically tinged pieces, this particular project and much of the symbolism seems to come to a rather abrupt halt by 1943, coincidentally around the time of Colquhoun's marriage to Toni del Renzio.

Perhaps this experimental work was as much about pain as it was

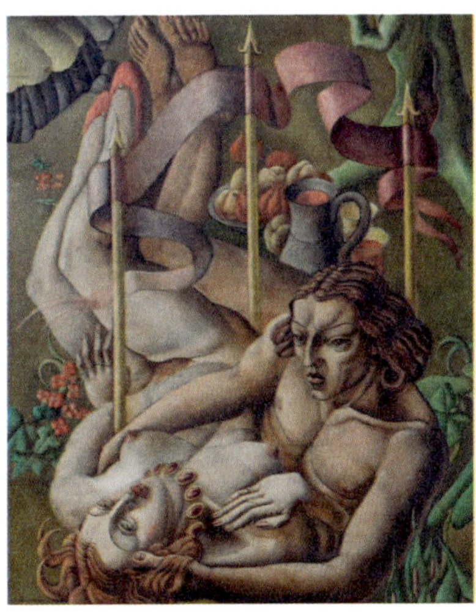

about pleasure. Colquhoun's own erotic gaze buffers between desire and a detached objectivity. Is her experimental sensibility in some way distancing her from her own desires? The collection is an interesting and highly explicit focus on disembodied parts, moments of arousal, bodies as instruments and potentialities. That Colquhoun appears to have inserted herself into many of these sketches with lovers who were male, female and perhaps not even human, shows the way that she moved between the subjective and the objective, making it both a project for human evolution and also very clearly a way of confronting her own sexuality.

Yet in today's cultural context of renavigating gender, sex and the bodies and spaces we inhabit, Colquhoun's work has new relevance. The excavation of the once ubiquitous yet now nearly forgotten sacrality of the androgyne in esoteric and occult culture, speaks to new generations yearning to escape labels and containers that confine us all. So, while Colquhoun's work may be infused with the echoes of her own struggles, along with notes of passion, beauty and desire, at the core of this project seems to be hope – a hope that each of us individually and the world we live in can come closer to some sense of wholeness, awakening the divinity which dwells within us all.

Song of Songs 1933
Oil paint on canvas
86 × 72.5
Courtesy Unit London

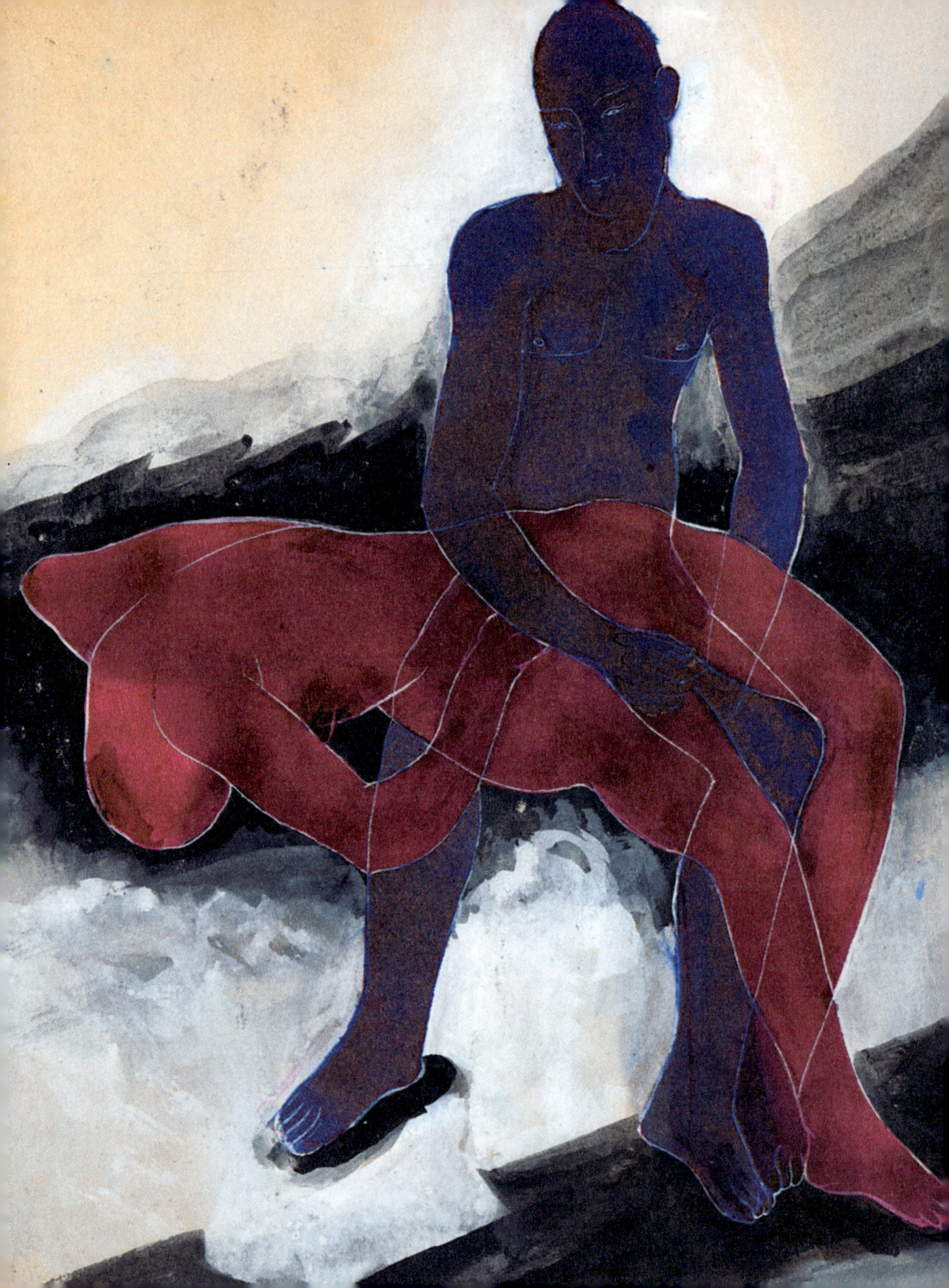

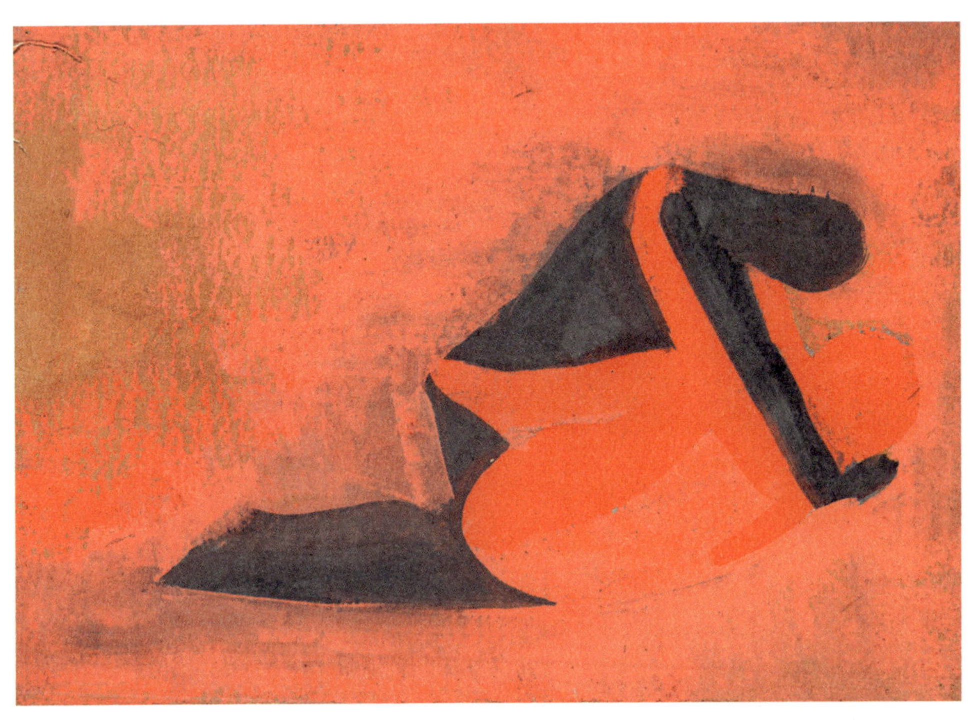

*Untitled painting of magenta
and indigo couple* c.1940–2
Watercolour on paper

*Untitled painting of red and
indigo couple* c.1940–2
Watercolour on paper

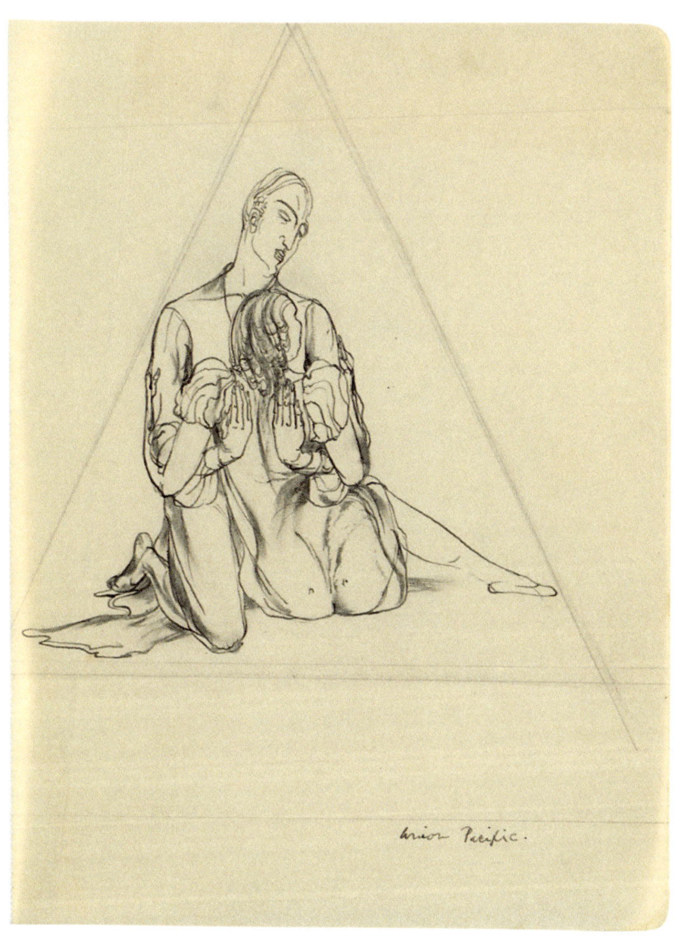

Untitled sketch of Union Pacific c.1940–2, pen and graphite on paper

28

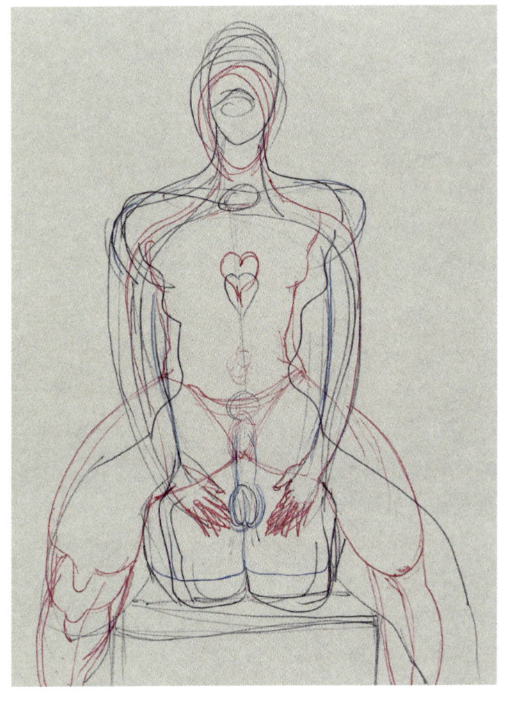

Figure/lovers c.1940–2
Pen on paper, 26.5 × 20.1

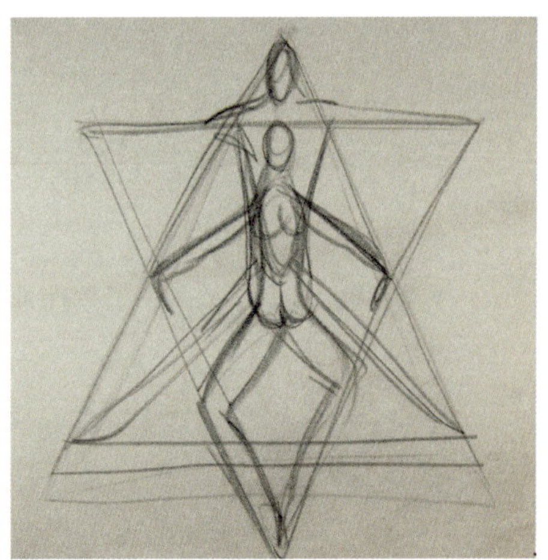

*Untitled sketch of couple
in hexagram formation*
c.1940–2
Graphite on paper

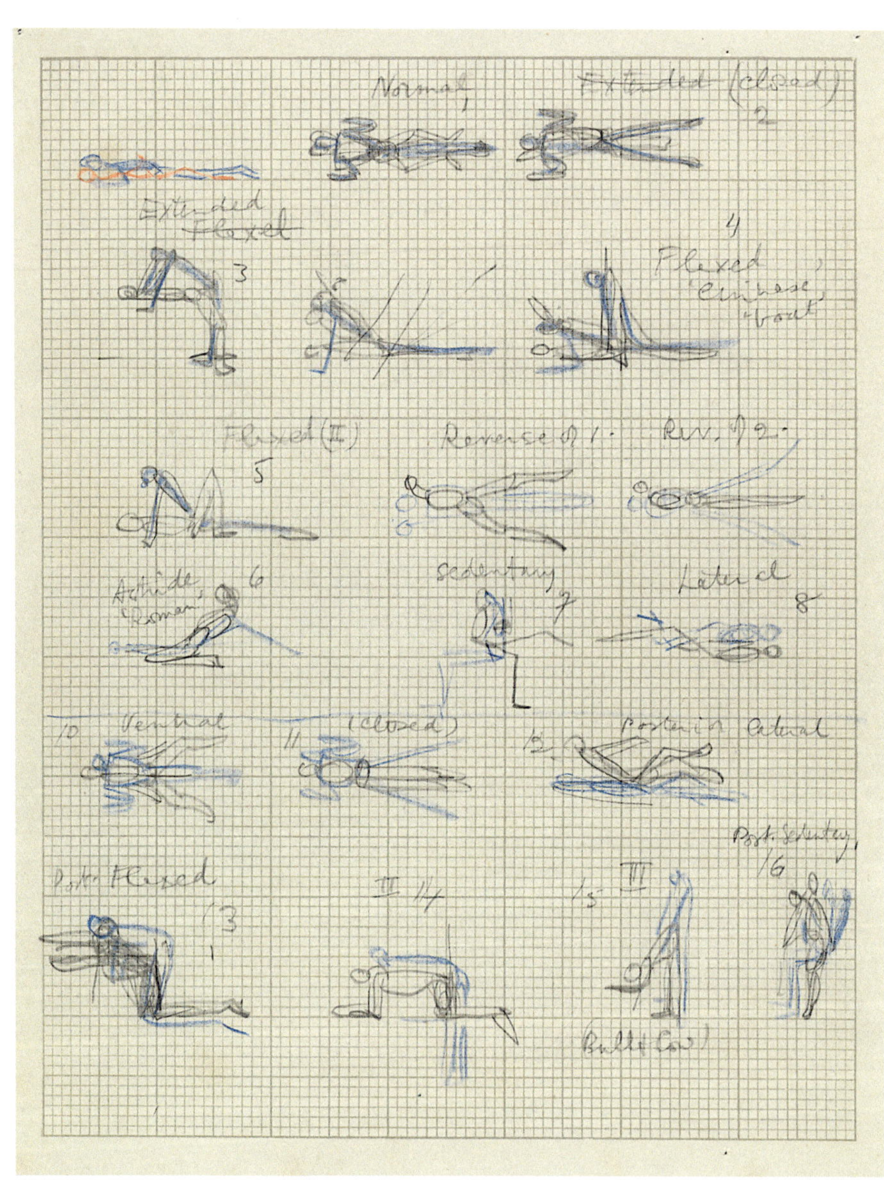

Untitled diagram showing
sketches of sexual positions
c.1940–2, pen on graph paper

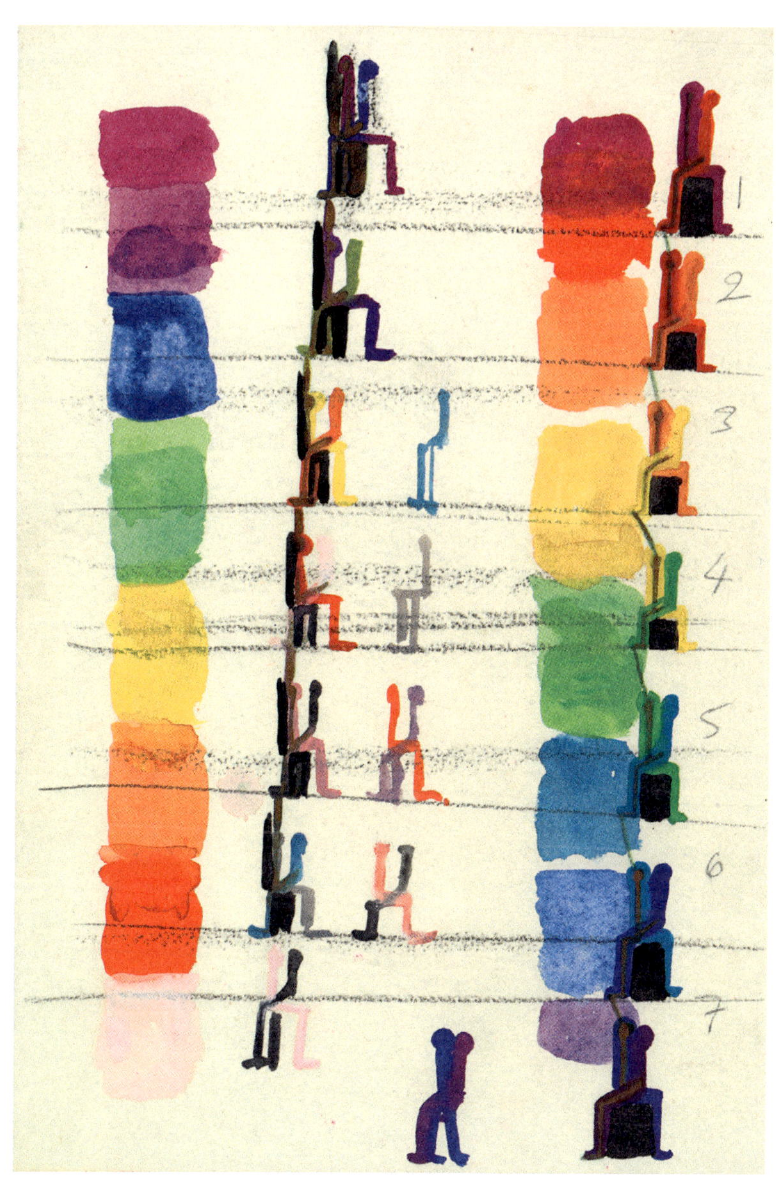

Colour Key of couples
c.1940–2, graphite and
watercolour on paper

Love Charm I

Messengers, listen to me!
Take him the symbols he understands
Here is a dove, a swan
A lynx leading the tribe of cats
A garden with clover
Honey, a grove of myrtle
An apple tree, the opening flower of a rose
Benzoin, red sandalwood, the soft odours
I give him the drug damiana, drink!
The image of a doorway
And all enclosed in a girdle.

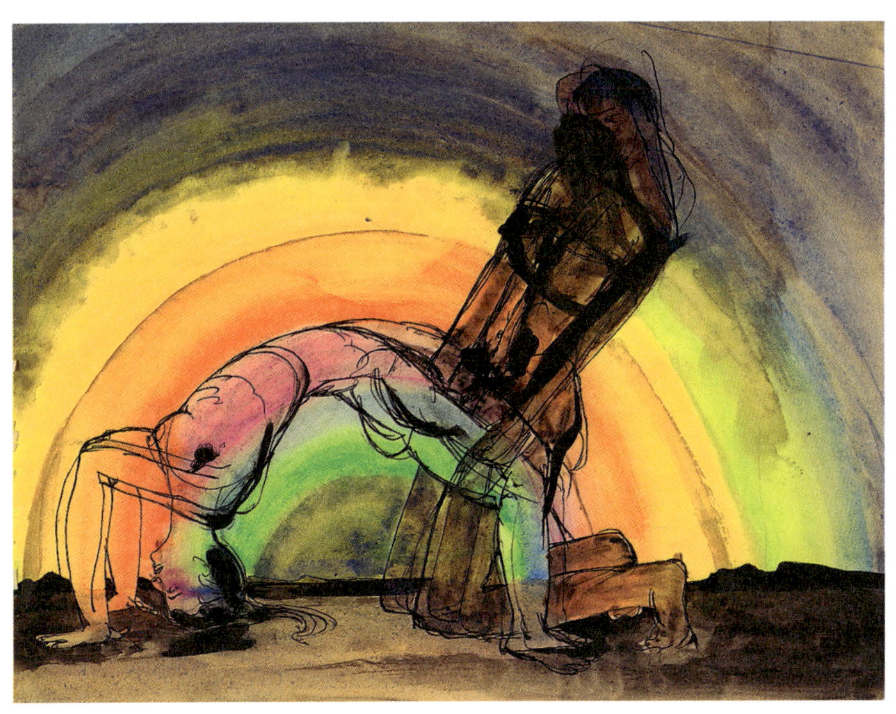

*Untitled painting of
conjoined couple with
rainbow* c.1940–2
Watercolour and pen
on paper

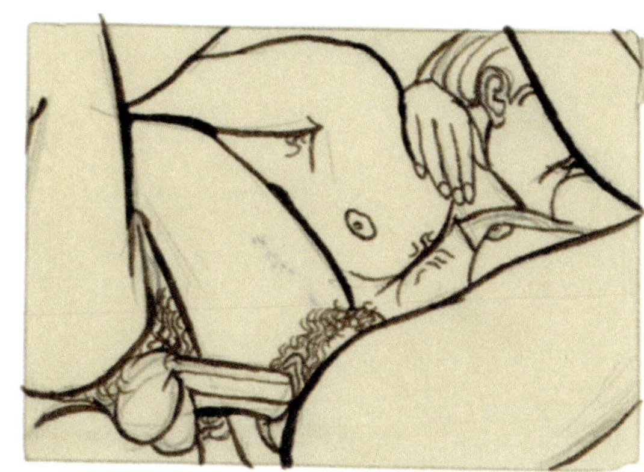

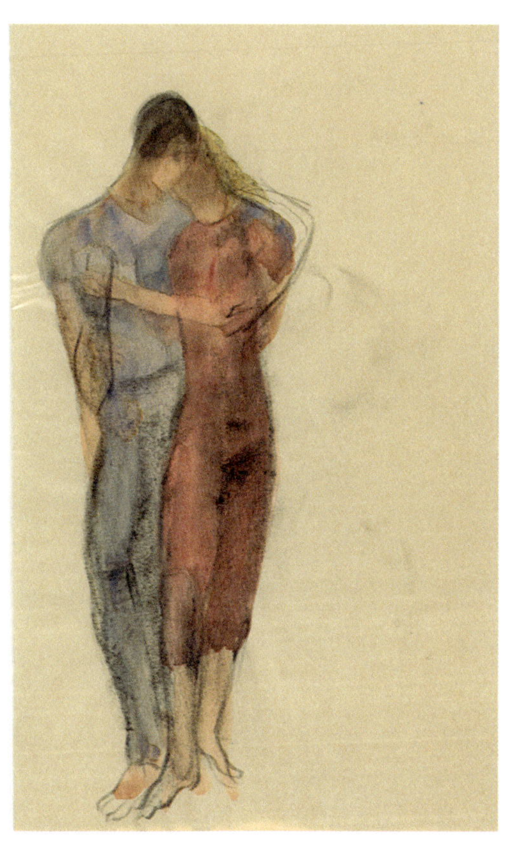

*Untitled sketch of couple
kissing in red and blue
garments* c.1940–2
Graphite and
watercolour on paper

*Untitled sketch of
penetration* c.1940–2
Pen and ink on paper

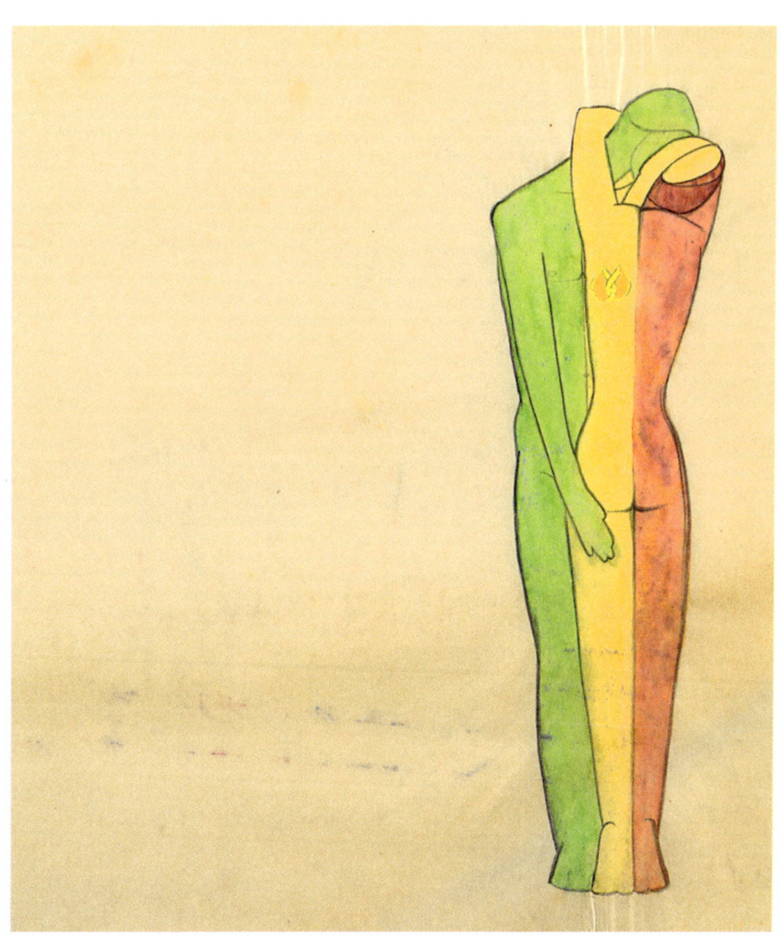

Embracing Couple in Red, Yellow and Green 1940, watercolour on paper, 13 × 18.2

35

Love Charm II

I write with the unfading ink
Used for a declaration
A record not to be falsified.

I invoke the parts of the body
In their planetary connections
From the head dedicated to Mars
To the feet in Jupiter
Zenith to nadir
I assign them all to Venus' work
Until we possess one another.

Sigils of the grimoire you I recall
Constructing the pantacle of protection
I make the gestures, speak the words

I call on left and right
I call on north and south
I call on night and day
I call on the two halves of the year
I conjure into Venus' pantacle, there to stay
Until we possess one another.

I summon from the collective dream
Symbols of the magian world
To do my will under Venus' sign:

I summon salt and sulphur
I summon mercury and gold
I summon diamond and ruby
I summon lymph and blood
I summon serpent and lion
I summon white tincture and red
I summon the tree bearing moon and sun as fruit
I put you under Venus' reign
Until we possess one another.

The vessel is ready:
Phoenix, here the alembic
Alchemy's firebird, light the furnace here!

Venus, bring a happy conjunction
At an auspicious hour
Bring the word and the touch
Bring coalescence of colours
Bring the coruscating sphere.
Bring the night of gold.

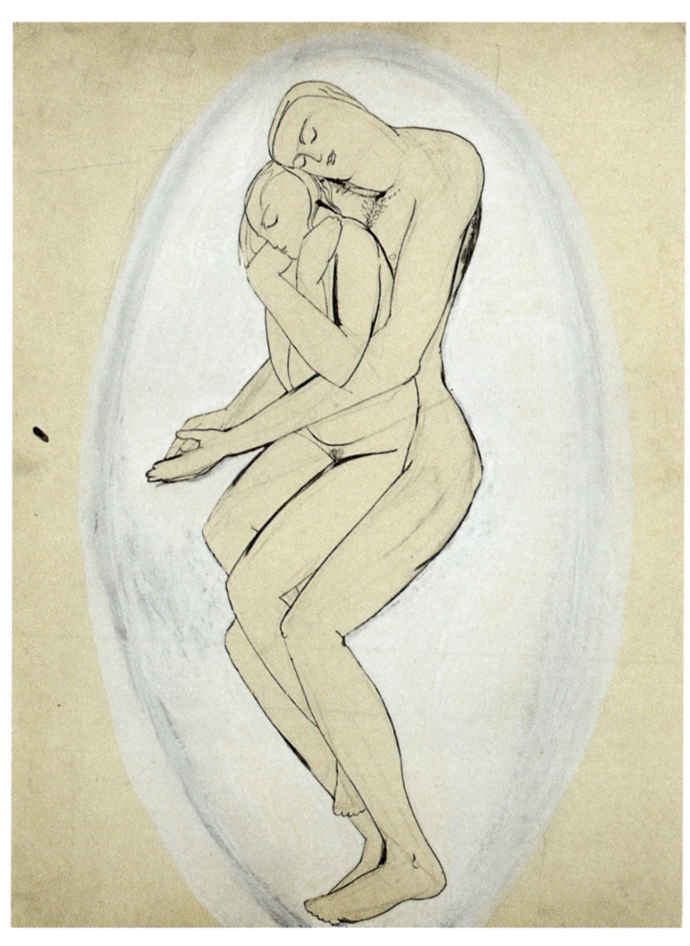

*Untitled sketch of a couple
embracing in an egg*
c.1940–2, graphite and
watercolour on paper

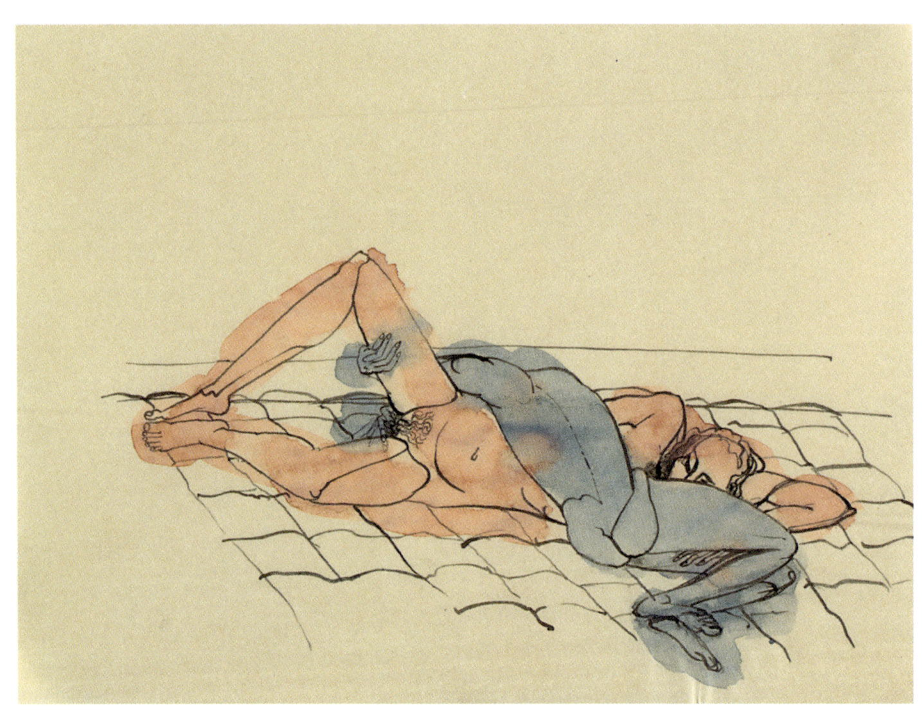

*Untitled sketch of pink
and blue couple entwined*
c.1940-2, ink and
watercolour on paper

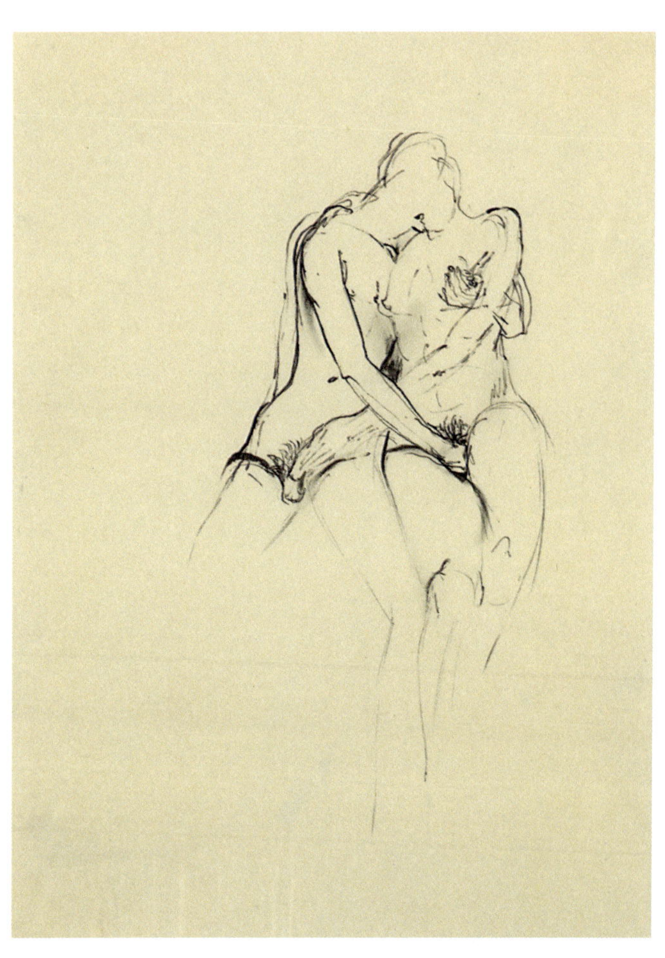

*Untitled sketch of couple
caressing* c.1940–2
Ink on paper

Possessed

You in the headdress
You in the robe
What did I drink
From your glass like a horn?

The taste was honey
The touch was oil
The colour was amber
But if it were these

Why did I fall
In so deep a swoon
Why am I drunk
After all this time?

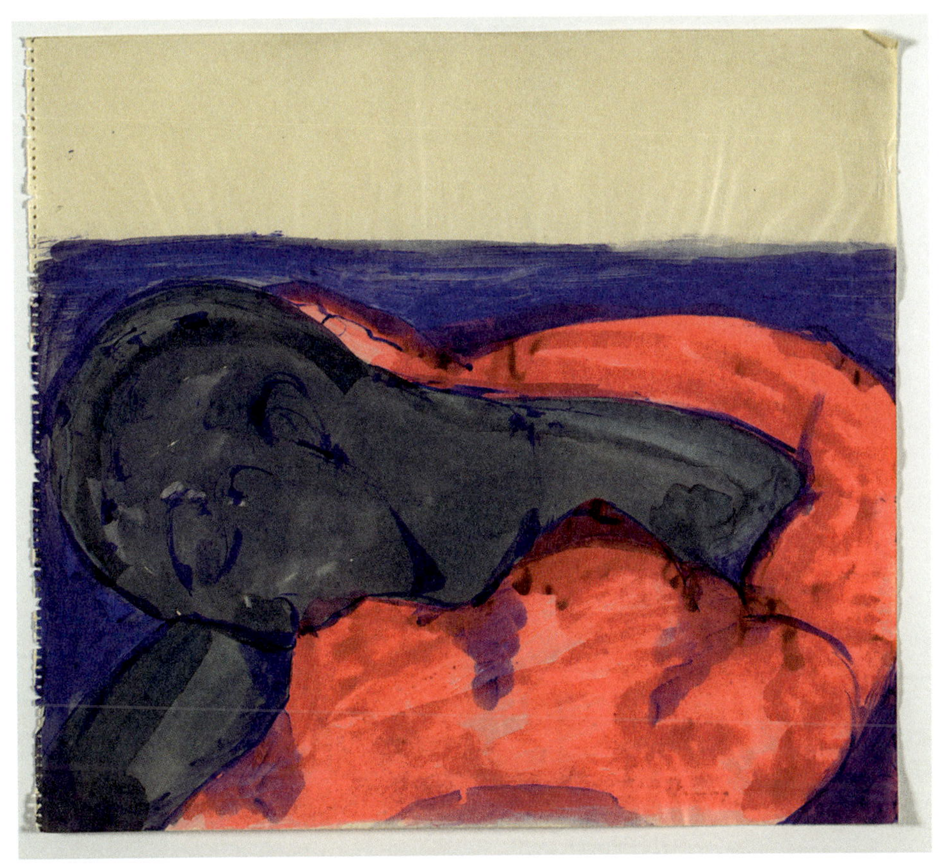

*Untitled painting of pink
and indigo couple no.3*
c.1940–2, watercolour
and pen on paper

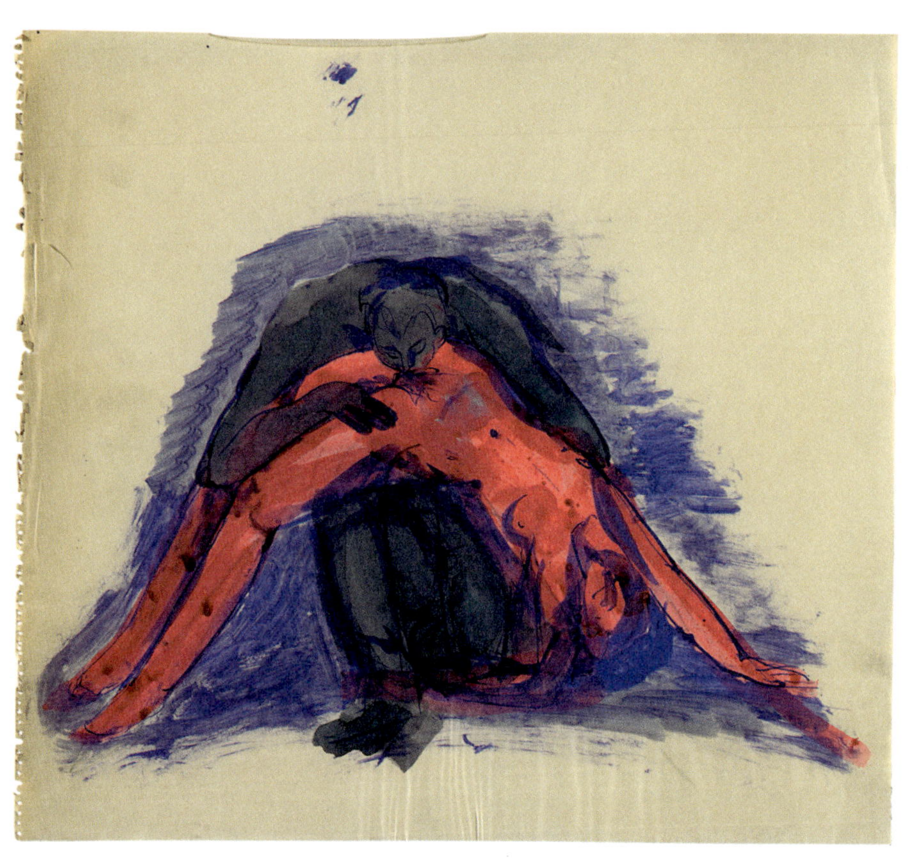

*Untitled painting of pink
and indigo couple no.1*
c.1940–2, watercolour
and pen on paper

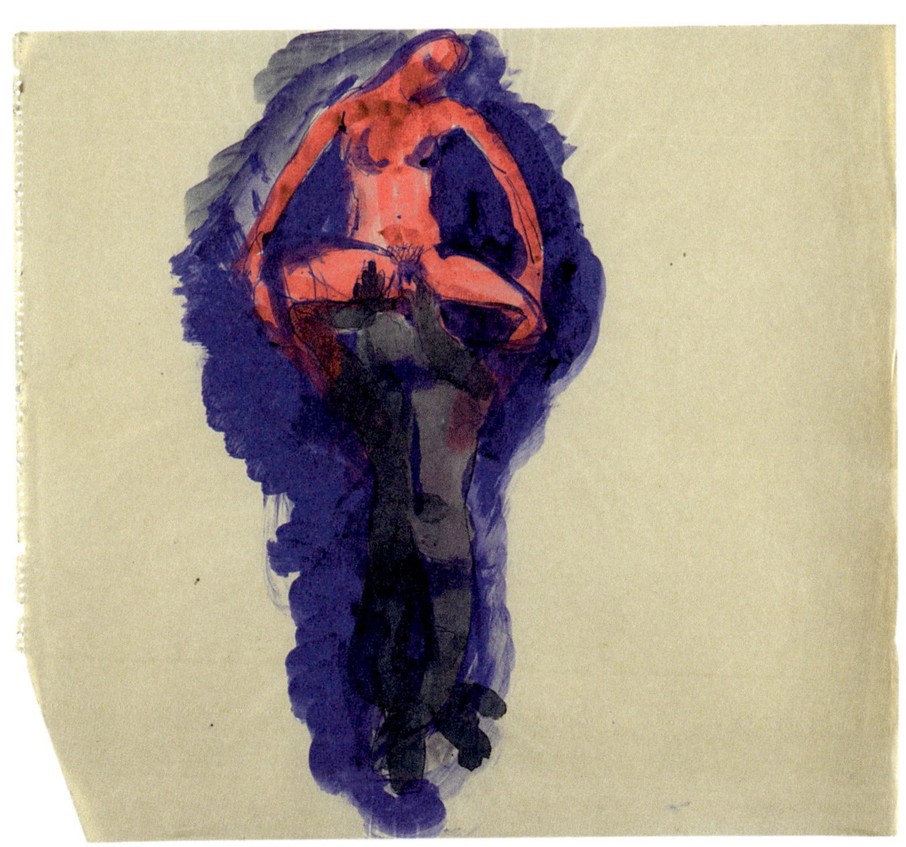

*Untitled painting of pink
and indigo couple no.2*
c.1940–2, watercolour
and pen on paper

43

Union Pacific

Proclaim the supersensual truth
That gods have limb and eye
Each with a counterpart
These pairs exultant cry
Ringing through the Universe
Announces victory

It is antimony resolved
Inspires their cosmic play
Having perfected dissonance
Nor mind nor body stray
But complete their echoed selves
Through aeons that are a day

Making celestial music
Their joy is to create
The everlasting instant in
An everlasting fate
Harmony in a double self
That needs not generate

As in a glow serenely
The two parts of the soul
Meet in angelic couplings
Hermaproditic whole
While from their incandescent point
The spaces outward roll

So in a natural image
A tree's boughs embraced
Will closely grow together
Fibres so interlaced
That by a breeze's motion
Their pleasure's moods are spaced

Why then exists division
Philosophers have asked
Division is life's substance
And may not here be masked
But though divided each can be
A chrysalis encasqued.

That opens to a dragonfly
Sunning a scarlet hue
To call another of its kind
But of cerulean blue
Or if it be cerulean
Follow a scarlet clue

And head-to-tail ecstatic float
Continuously one
Lyrical creatures to enjoy
So long a union
That they become a new being
Scarlet-cerulean.

These the self-same colours
The alchemists have shown
Lying in the alembic
Thalamus and throne
And have called them the opal
The stone that's not a stone

Where in tranquil burning
The solved antimony
Garnet with clear smaragdus
Are fused to unity
Sun and moon in opal lose
And keep identity

Moved from the dual center
Of a creative trance
Gods, men and insects, trees and stones
Take part in a dance
Where closer clasp the partners
Keener their pleasures lance

Within the unconsuming fire-
Loveliest o loveliest theme
Of every theme the elixir
This dance and trance proclaim
Quenched and rekindles is desire
In this triumphal dream.

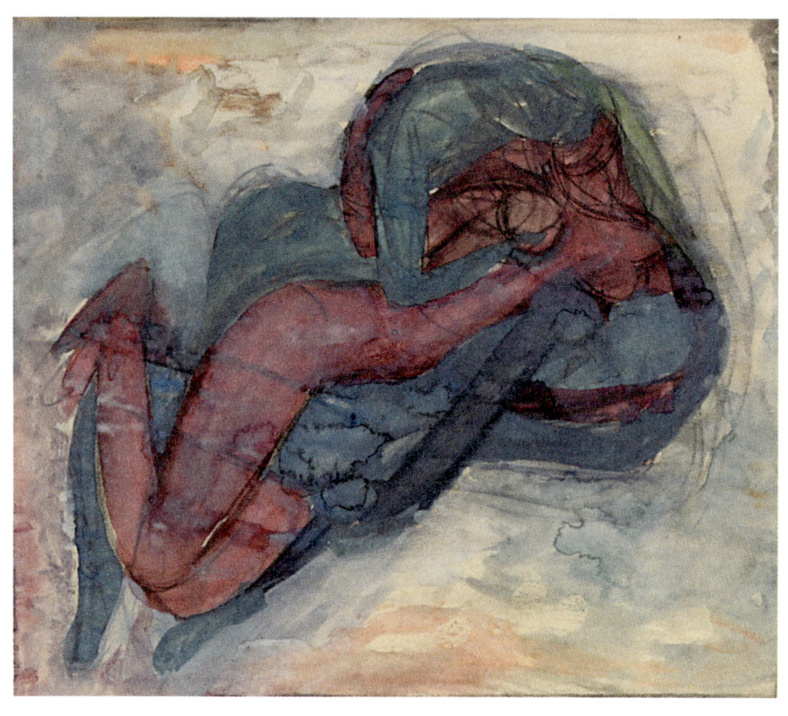

*Untitled sketch of three
figures embracing no.1*
c.1940–2, watercolour
on paper

*Untitled sketch of blue
and pink couple entwined,
'The Stone that is not a
Stone'* c.1940–2, ink and
watercolour on paper

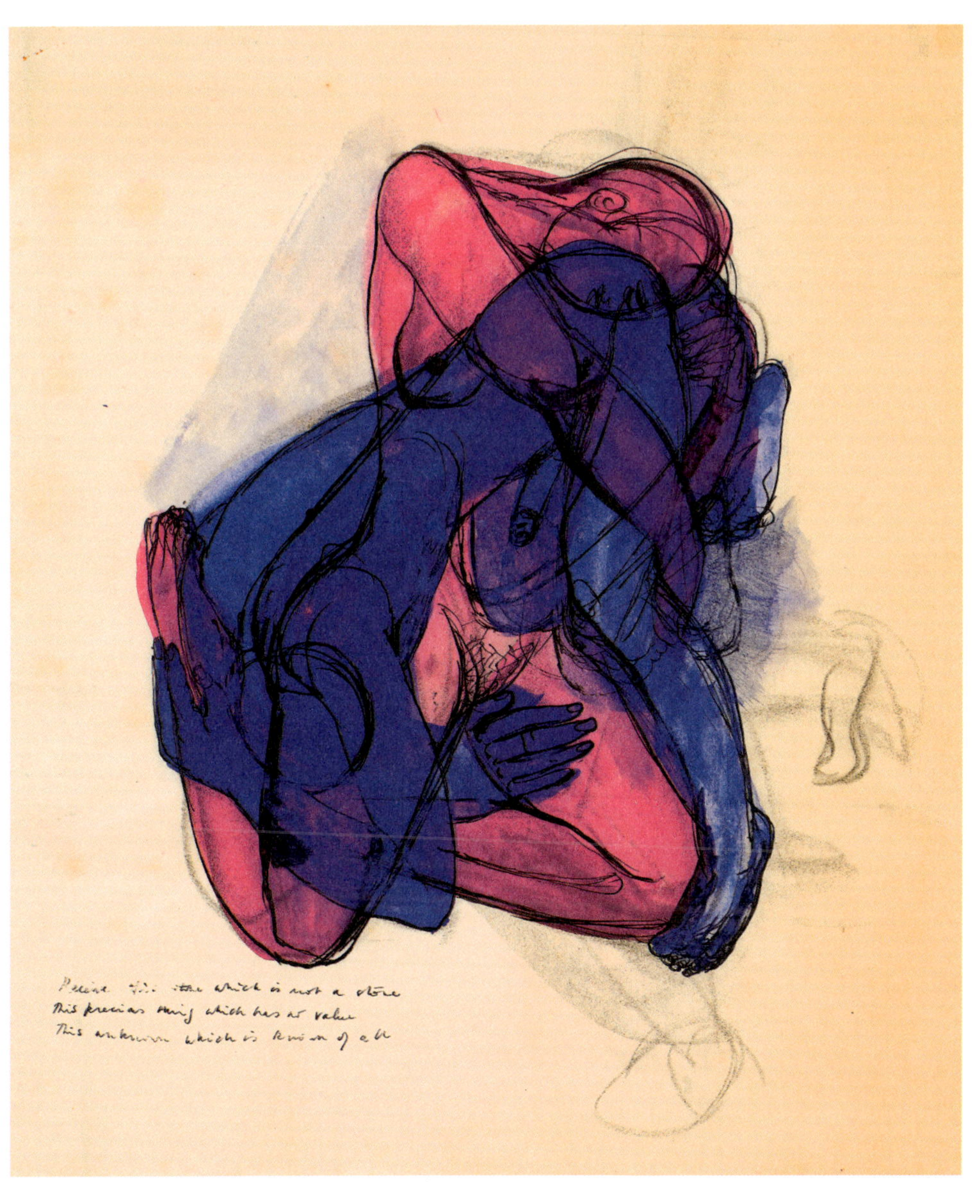

Receive this stone which is not a stone
This precious thing which has no value
This unknown which is known of all

Alchemical Figure:
Androgyne 1941
Watercolour on paper
23 × 37

Alchemical Figure
'Androgyne'
1941.

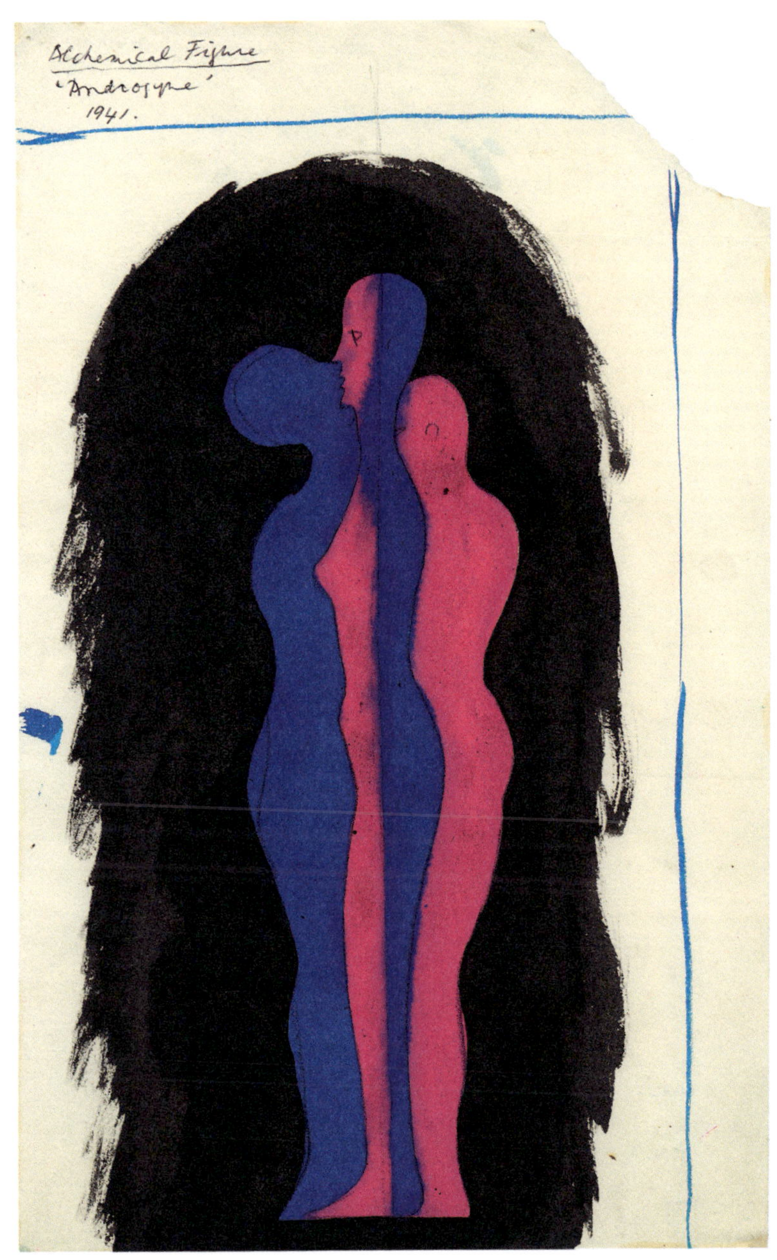

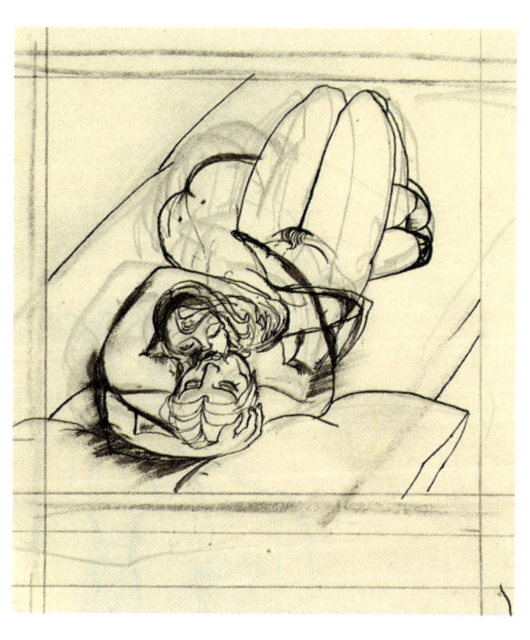

*Untitled sketch of two
women embracing*
Graphite on paper

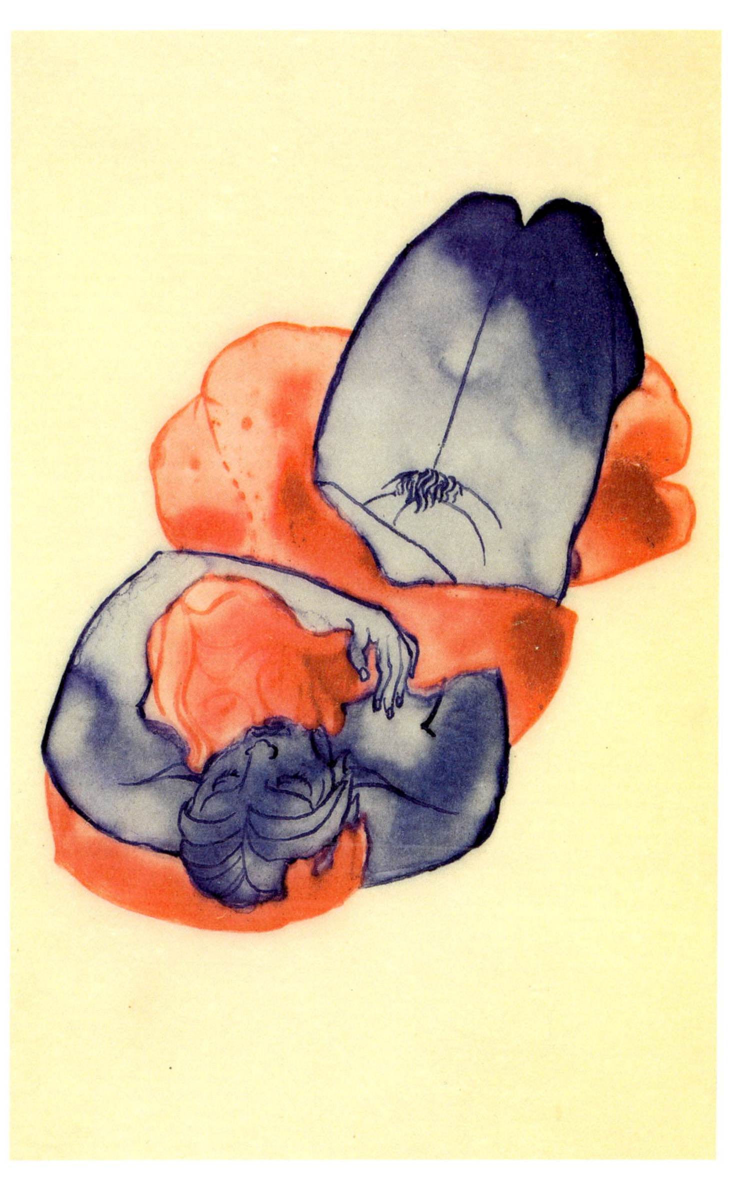

*Untitled painting of two
women embracing*
Watercolour on paper

Wedding of Shades

When the body becomes crystalline
It is the Bath of Venus

I think of him
And right and left my hands
Are full of rosy fire

I arrive like a ghost
I move like a roe
Eyes say nothing
Lips are blind
But the air tingles

A clear red
I bask in
Red of a wound
Red of health
His radiation

I that love clothes
Have to go naked
Not even my thigh
A jewel can wear
The night side of nature
Is my domain
Where darkness demands
The tryst unadorned

There were tigers wounds show
on the daylight body:
With no embrace there are bruises
on my thighs.

Enclosed by distance
As by a tower
I yield in trance
To a glowing shower
Origin
Of bloom on the skin

I am the untrodden path
Turning far back
That leads beside daylight
Unspoken word unlit moon
Flower unbreathed-on submerged plant
Star unreached-for
Crown of pearls.

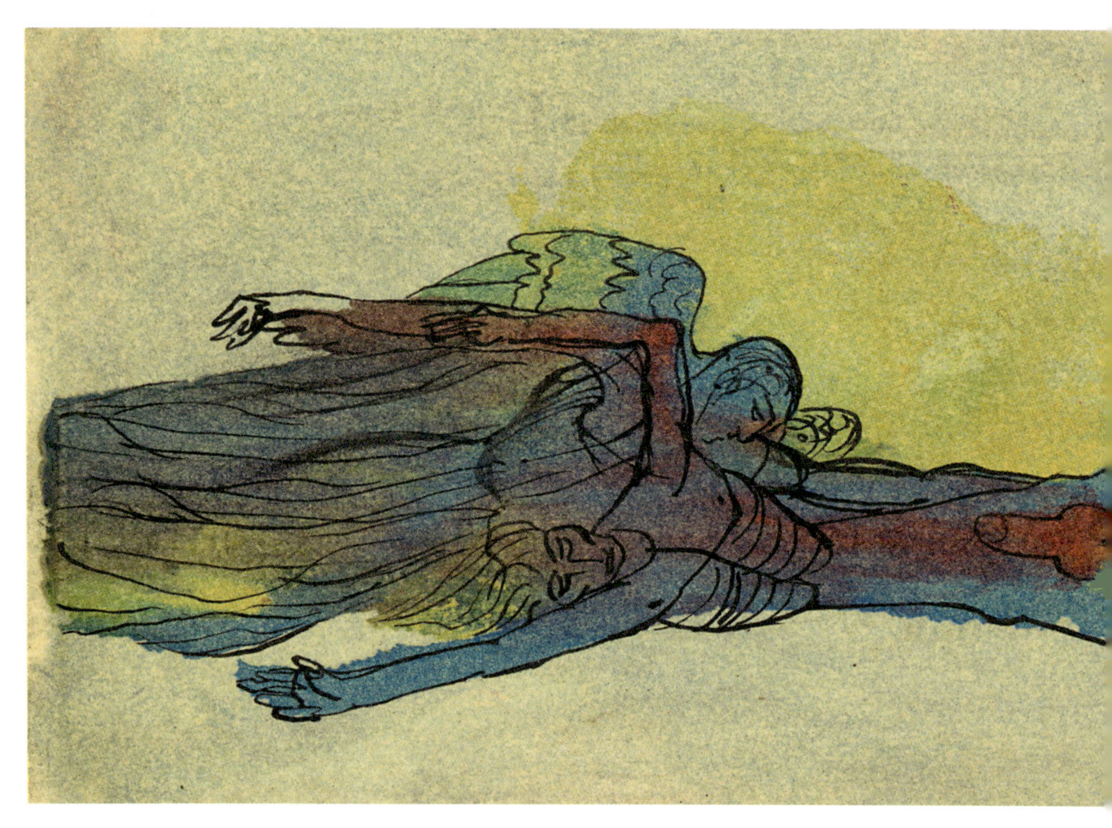

*Untitled painting of an
angel embracing a man*
Watercolour and ink on
paper

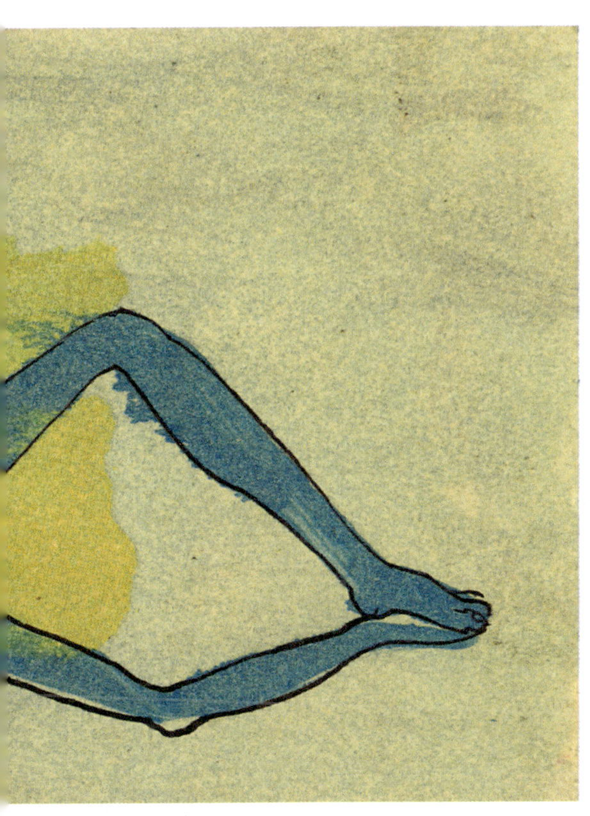

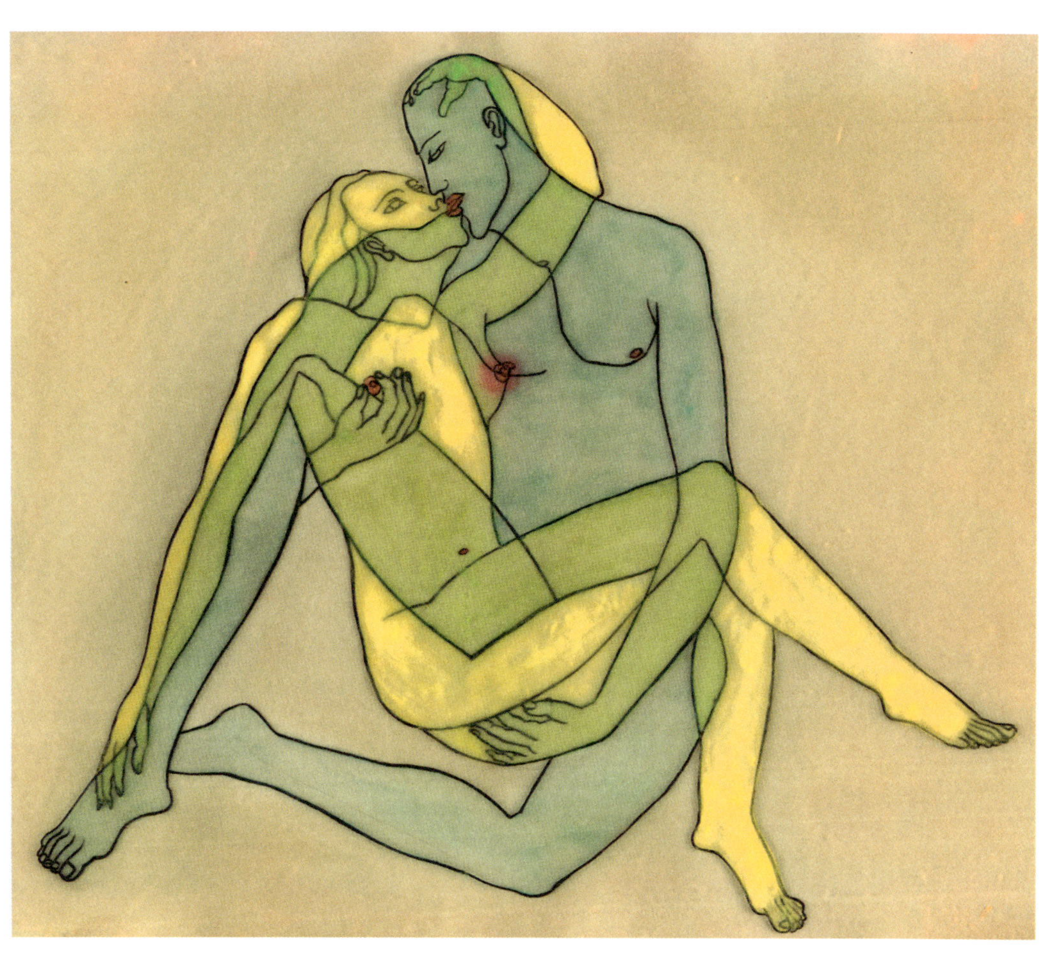

*Untitled work of green and
yellow couple embracing
no.1* c.1940–2
Ink on acetate

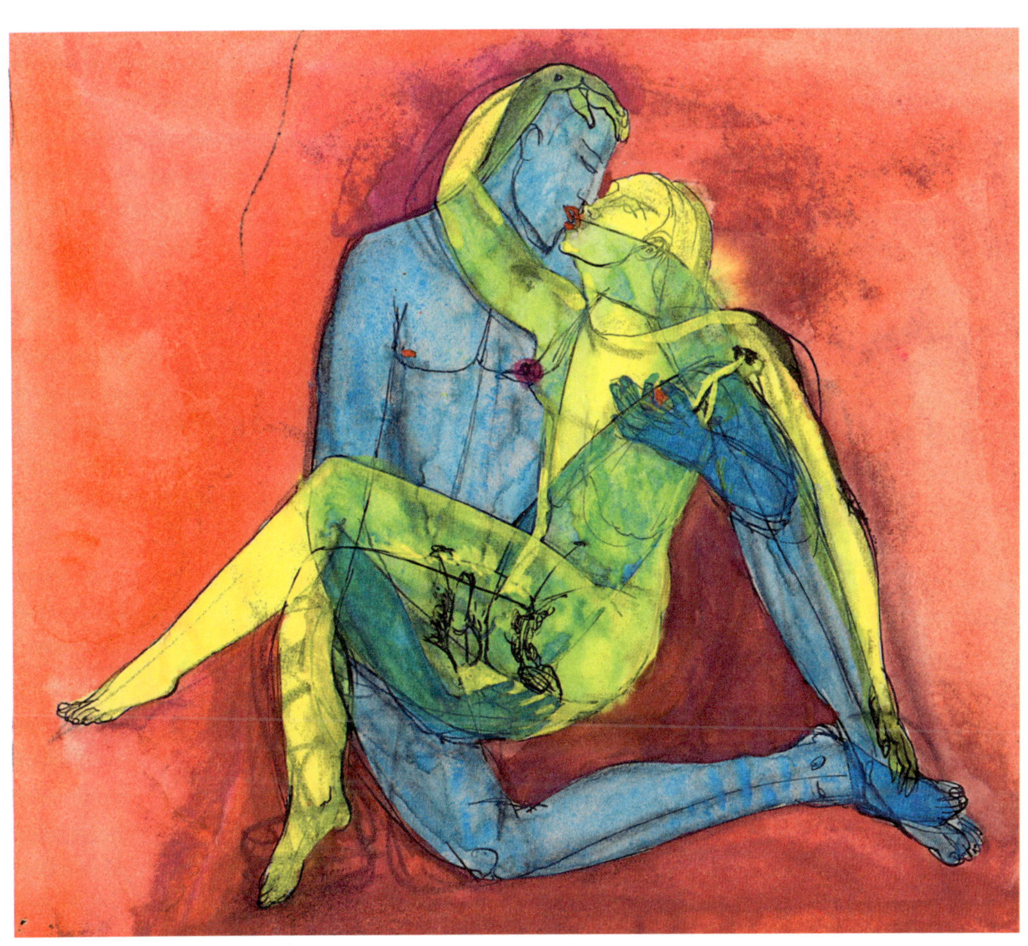

*Untitled painting of blue and
yellow couple embracing*
c.1940–2, graphite and
watercolour on paper

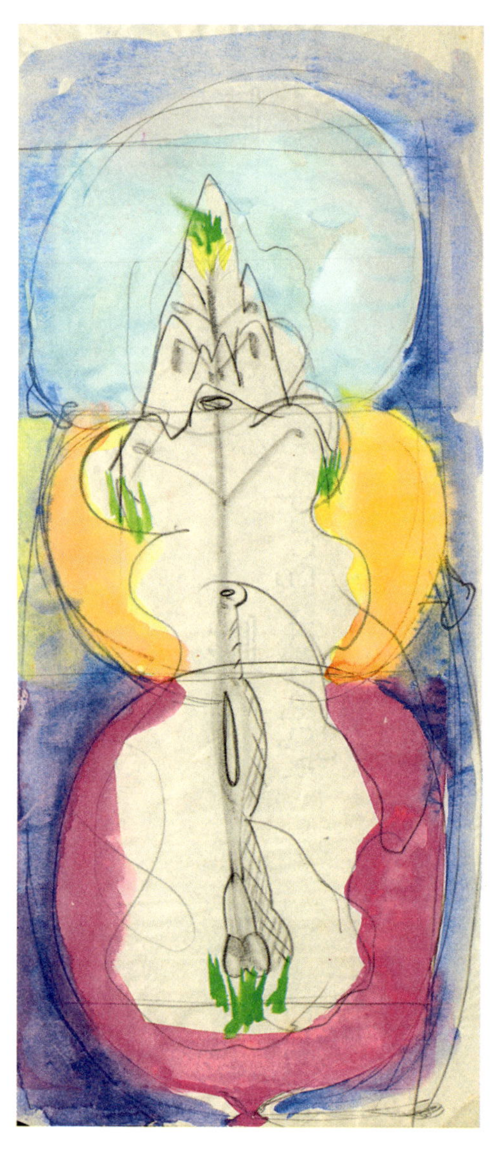

Untitled sketch of pink,
yellow and blue orbs with
phallus and mountains
c.1940–2, watercolour and
graphite on paper

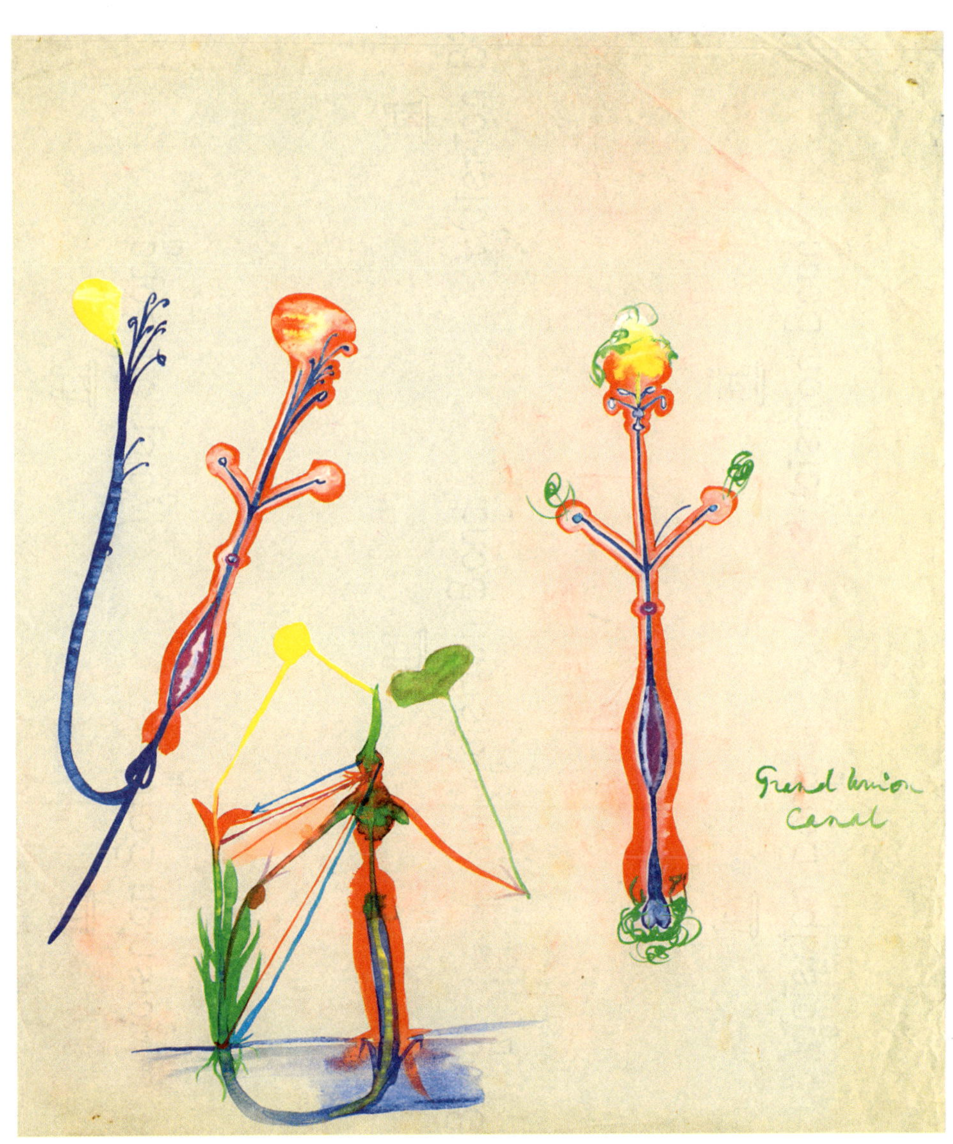

*Untitled sketches of Grand
Union Canal* c.1940–2
Watercolour on paper

Epithalamium

Air
Air of moon
Myself made perfect
Inmost sincerity

Earth
Earth of fire
Bone of the jaw, nourishment
That one, that one, he

Our sex is sealed
Each with a hexagram
Mutual symmetry

Bring us together
Earth in air
Ring us in
Blue circle of the air

*The Thirteen Streams of
Magnificent Oil* c.1940
Paint on tracing paper
20.5 × 32

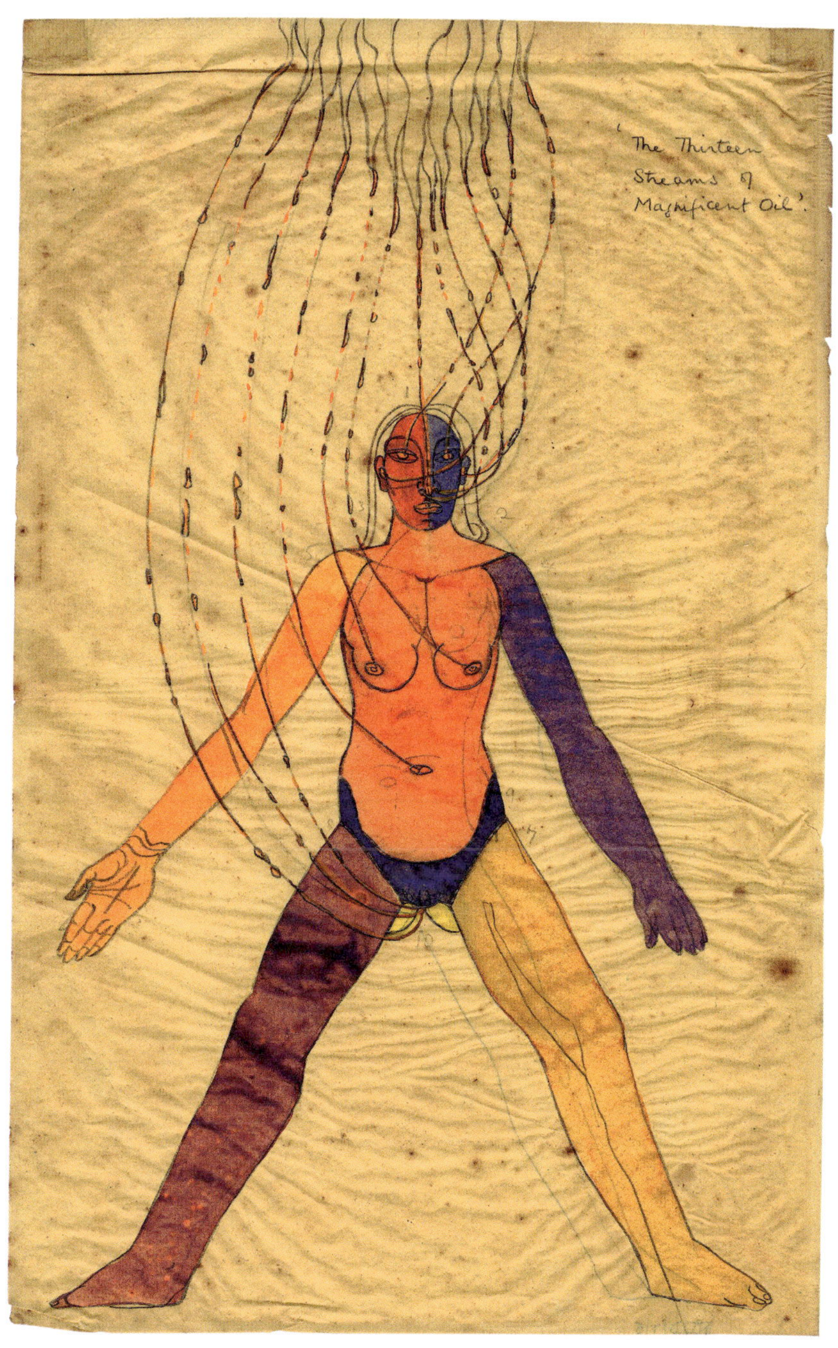
'The Thirteen
Streams of
Magnificent Oil'.

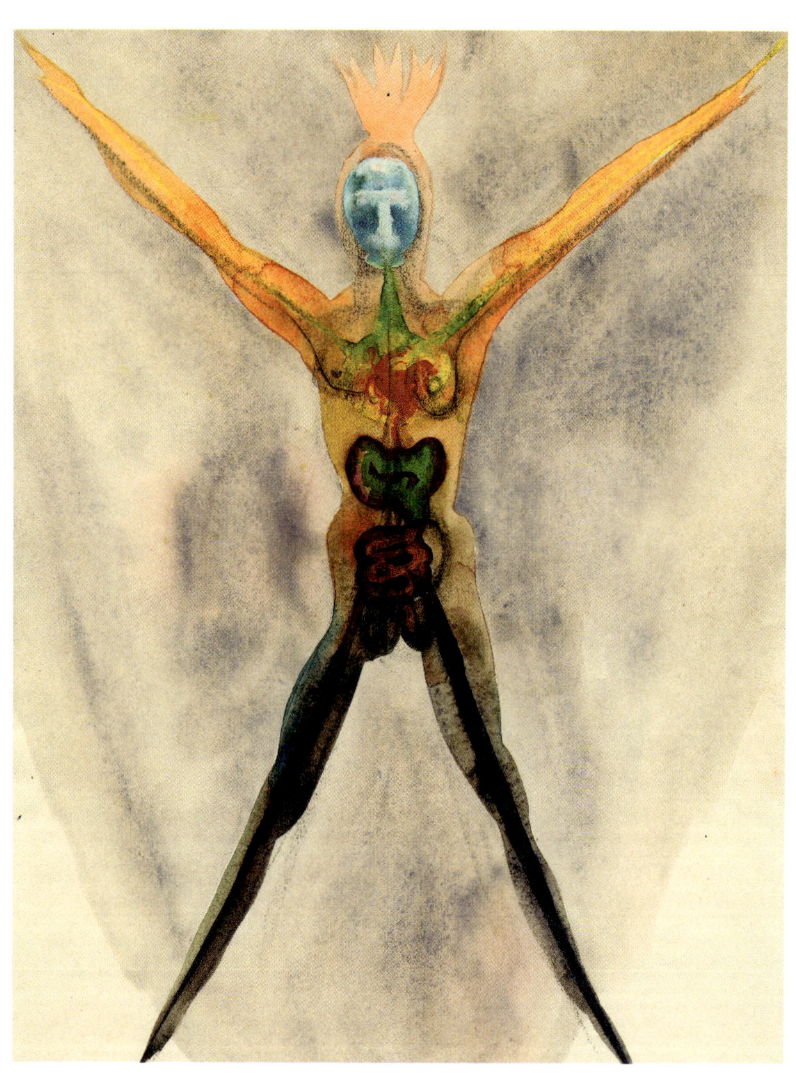

Alchemical Figure 1940
Watercolour on paper
25 × 36

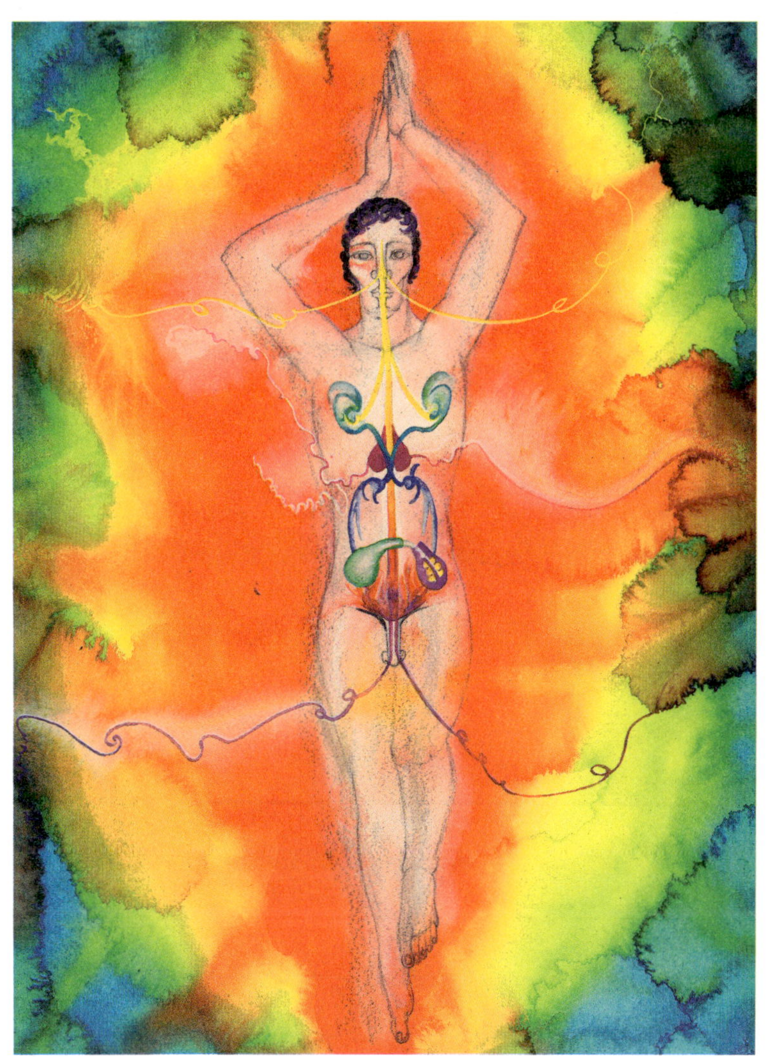

Second Adam c.1942
Watercolour and graphite
on paper, 32.5 × 46.5

63

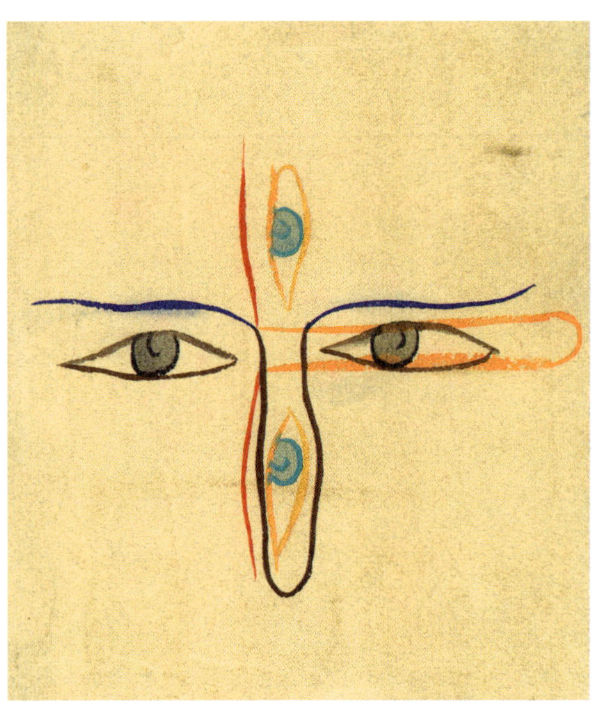

*Diagrams of Love: Marriage
of Eyes* c.1940–2
Pastel and ink on paper

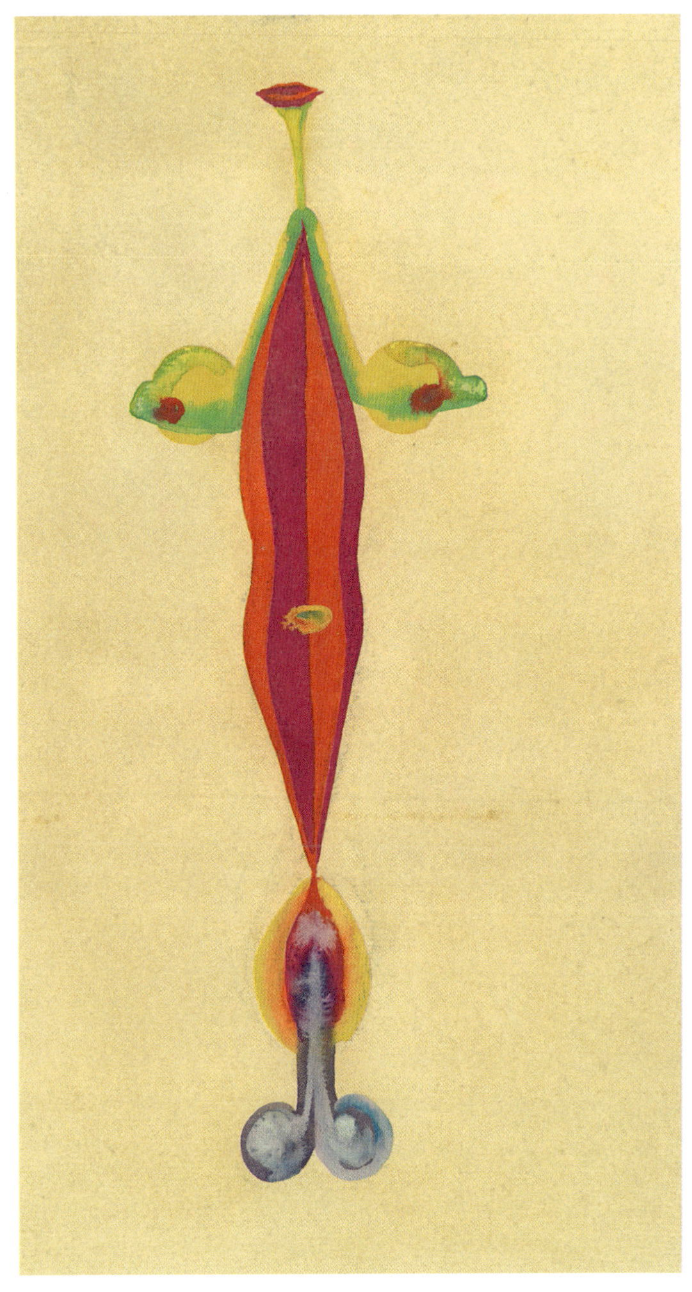

Diagrams of Love: The Androgyne I c.1940
Watercolour on paper
35 × 25.5

65

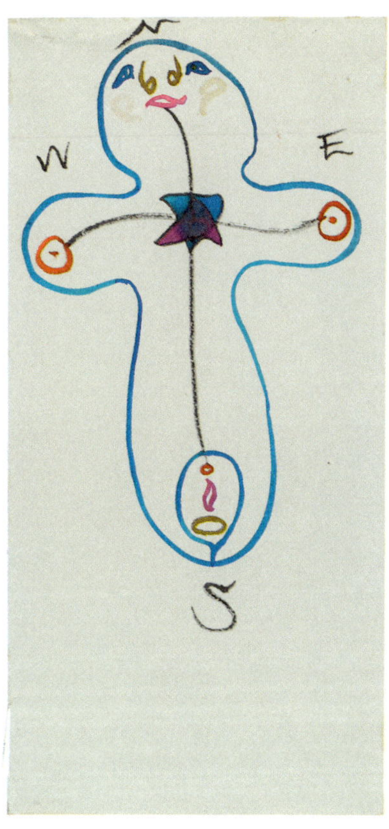

The Homunculus IV c.1940
Watercolour on paper
45.7 × 20.3

Machine for Conjuration
c.1940, watercolour on
paper, 27.9 × 20.2

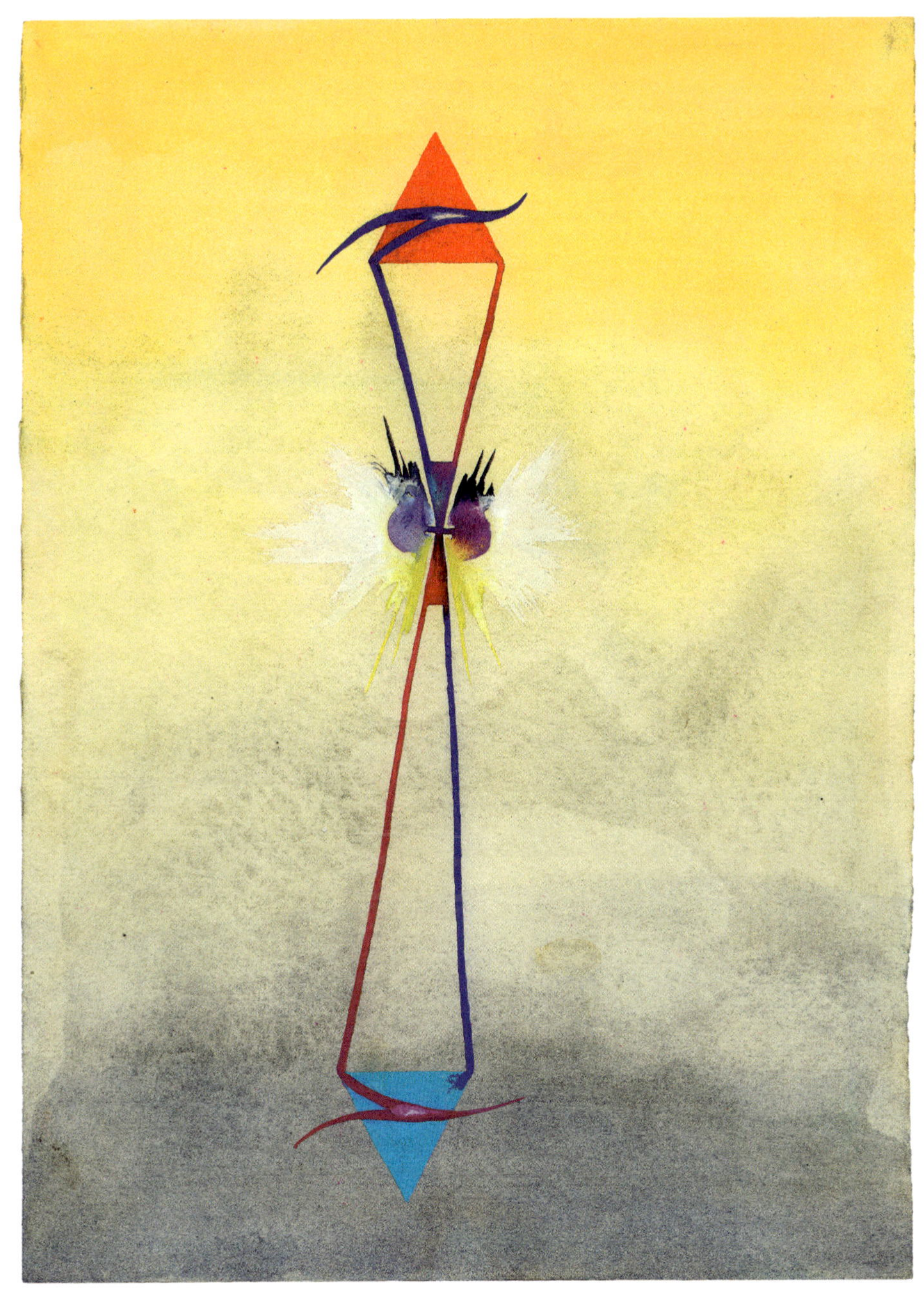

67

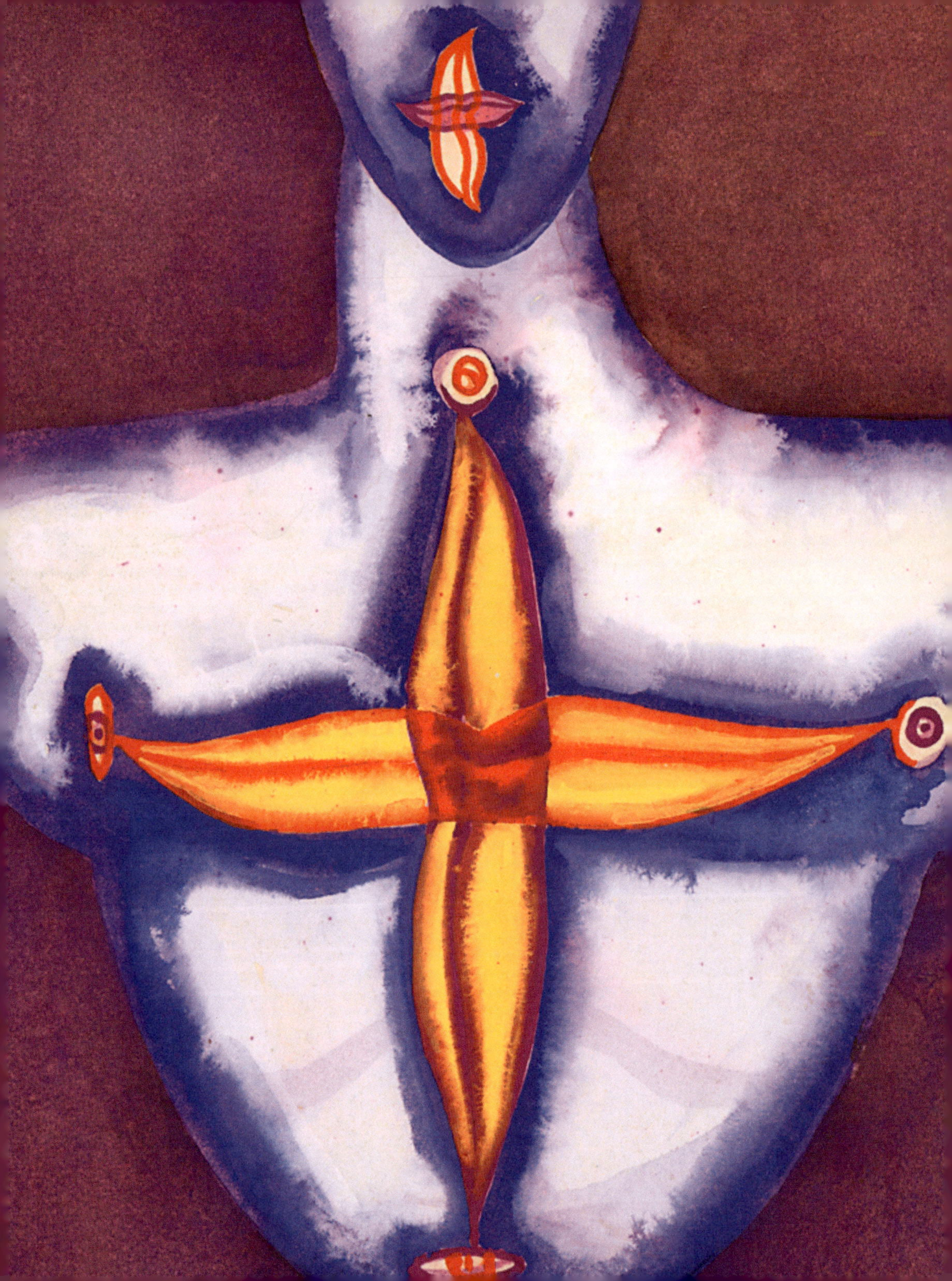

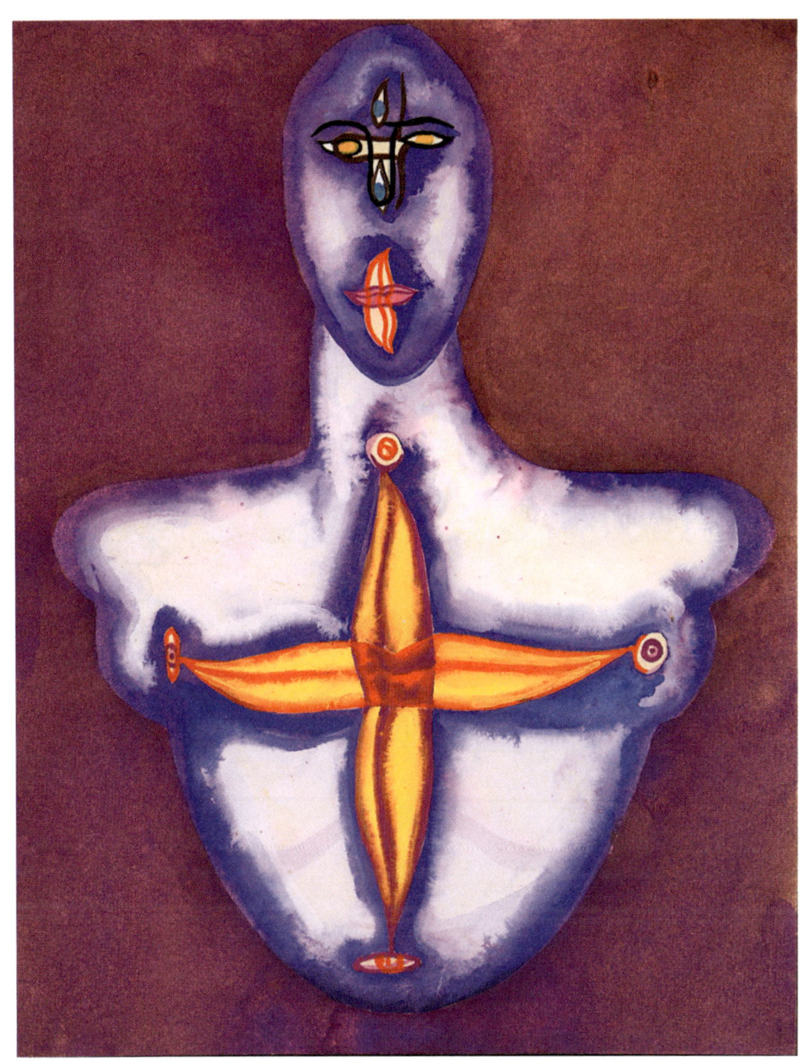

Christian Marriage I c.1942
Watercolour and graphite
on paper, 23 × 18.2

69

Diagrams of Love I

Every day
More deeply yet
Without the senses
Used for love
I grow to know you
In ways unknown

The plaited water
Of the midstream
Flows between us
Links and divides
Purple and red
Blood in circulation

The right eyelid
Is a sacred spot
Calf of the left leg
Should be bare
Wrists arms
Thighs groins
All were marked
With the same sign

There is a hollow
In your ribs
Where I lie

There is a hollow
In my ribs
Where you lock

Nothing can change this
But you may choose
An ill fitting chest
If you will

Every voyage to the realms of fire
Adds a flame to the wand
To the worlds of water each journey
A drop to the cup

Breast to magnetic breast
We drawn near in the odour of twilight
Laying the path we tread
Step by stone

I would be a
Sea anemone
Flower of tendrils
Opening into the
Current of love

Bells on a branch
Bright red buds
Drops on a wand, a whip

Under the sign of fire
I offer you red leaves
From the eucalyptus, the sound
Of trumpets, warmth, love

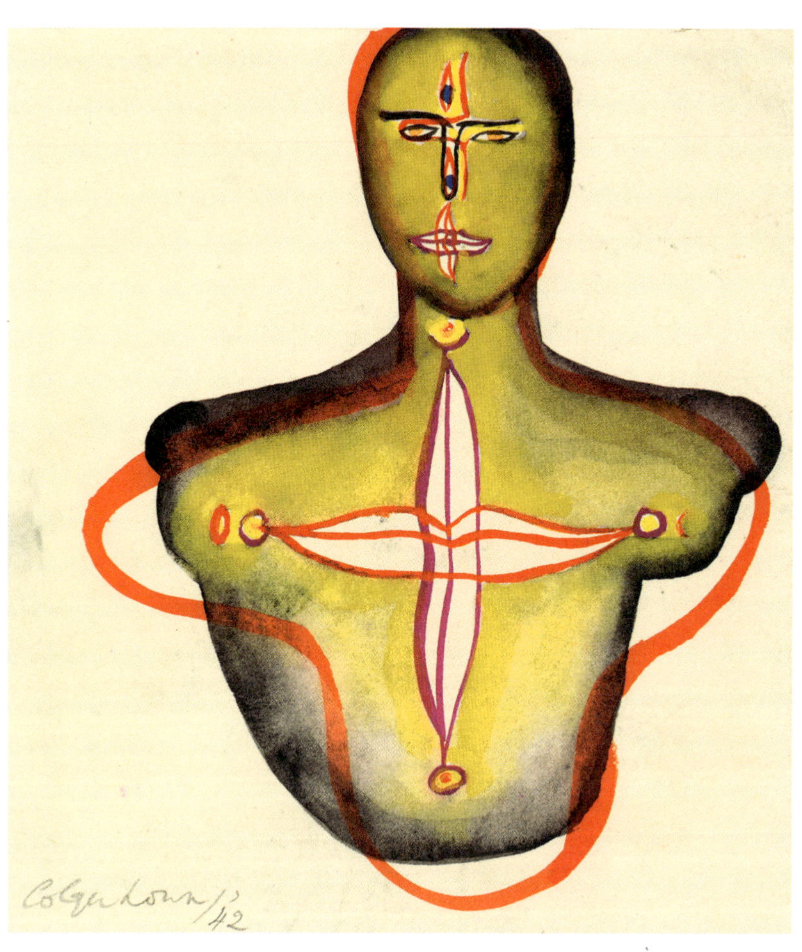

Christian Marriage Figure
1942, watercolour on
paper, 17.5 × 16

Christian Marriage II c.1942
Watercolour and graphite
on paper, 27.2 × 17.7

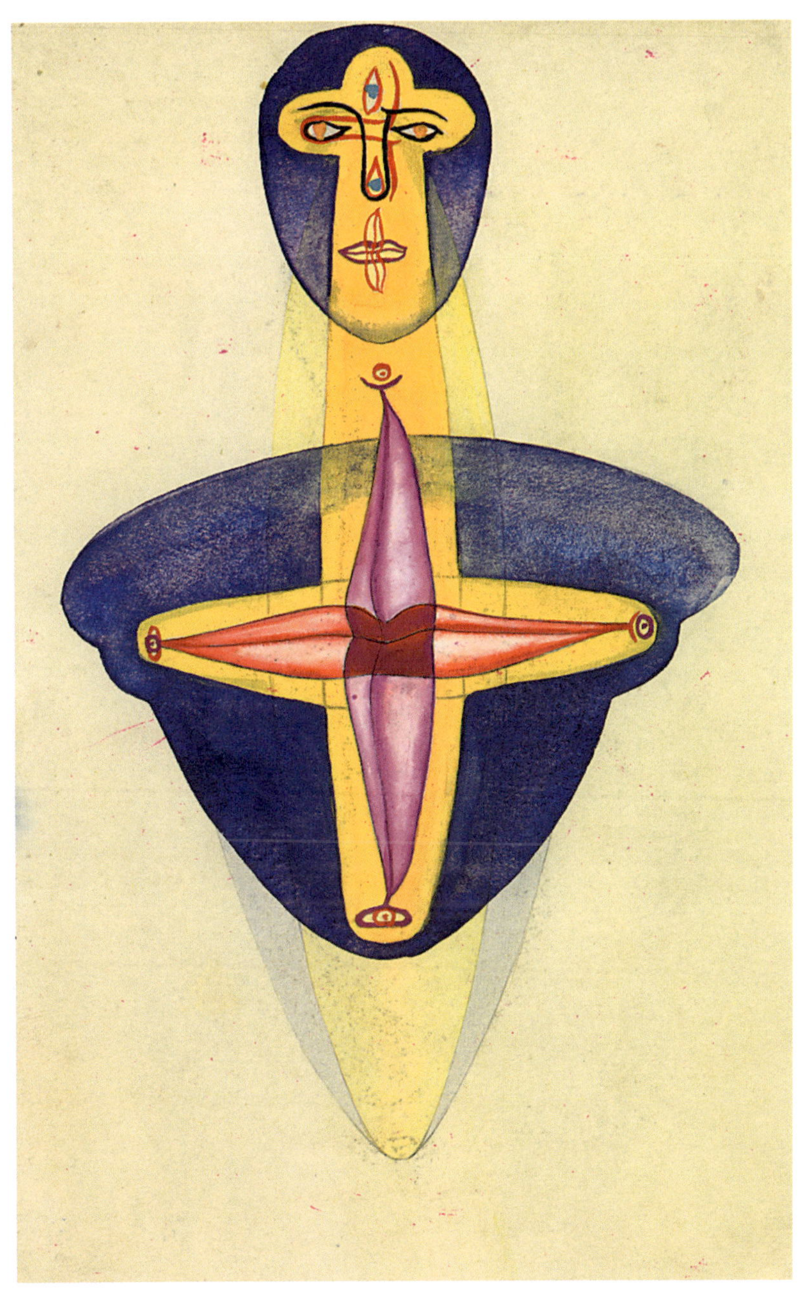

73

Diagrams of Love: The Bird
or The Egg? 1940–1
Watercolour on paper,
16.5 × 25.5

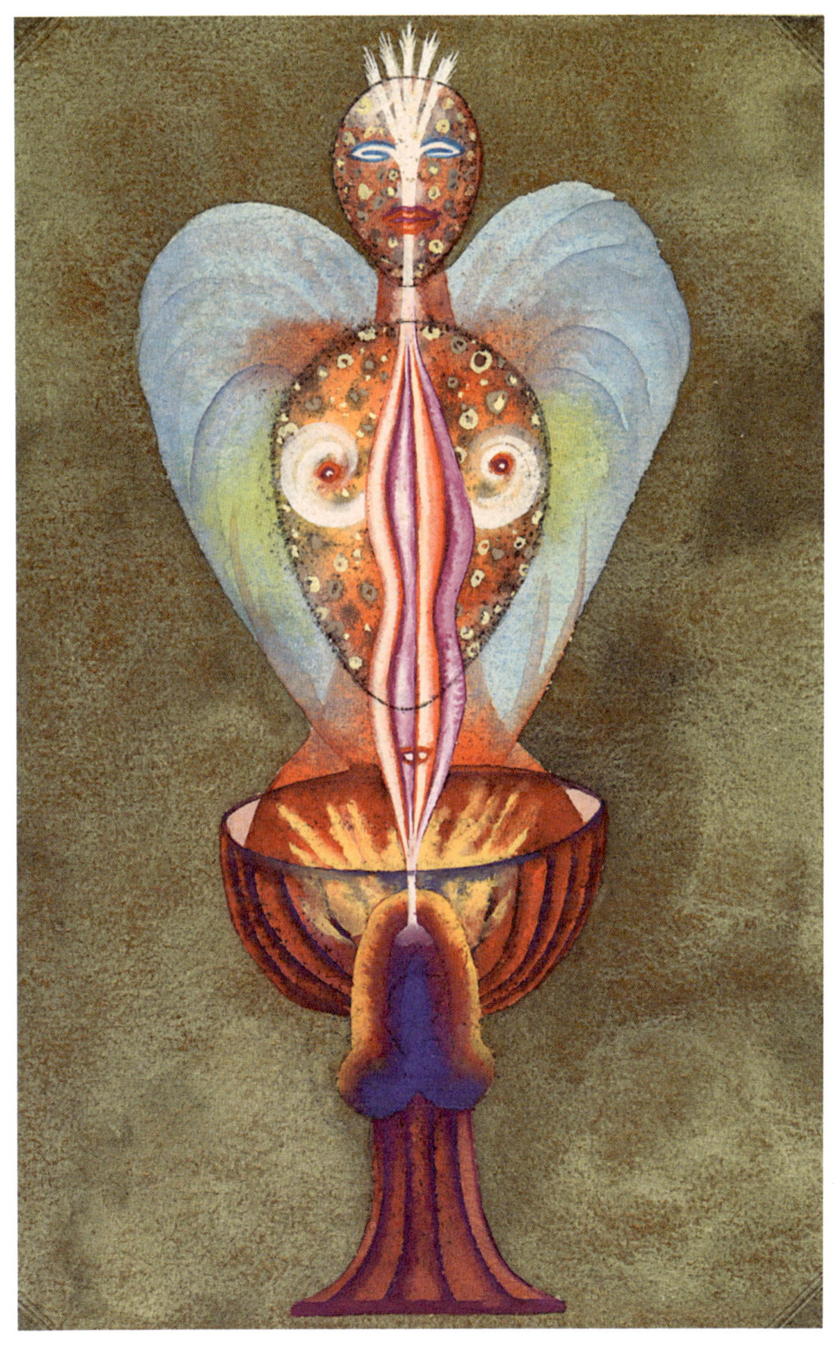

Anatomy Of Delight

Tell me my name says the head
Your name is the egg of forever
Tell us our name say the eyes
Your names are bdellium and onyx
Tell me my name says the mouth
It is called the eater of dreams
Tell us our name say the nostrils
It is the bearers of life
Tell us our name say the ears
You are called the concentrators
Tell me my name says the tongue
You are a sword

Tell us our name say the ribs
It is heart's cage
Tell me my name says the sternum
It is the place of the link
Tell us our name say the nipples
You are called the eyes of the breast
Tell me my name says the hair of the armpits
Your name is tendril of tree fern
Tell me my name says the hair on the chest
Your name is the wandering grass
Tell me my name says the heart
The unmoved

Tell me my name says the pelvis
You are called the glorious cup
Tell me my name says the phallus
It is the bird from the ash

Tell us our name say the testicles
You are called the armies of brass
Tell me my name says the scrotum
It is called the veil or the banner
Tell me my name says the pubic hair
It is the growth of the sea
Tell me my name says the anus
Sea anemone.

Tell us our name say the arms
It is strength
Tell us our name say the hands
Your name is the skilled
Tell us our name say the legs
You are called the swift
Tell us our name say the feet
You are the well-founded
Tell me my name says the skin
Your name is crystalline dew
Tell me my name says the spine
It is crystal.

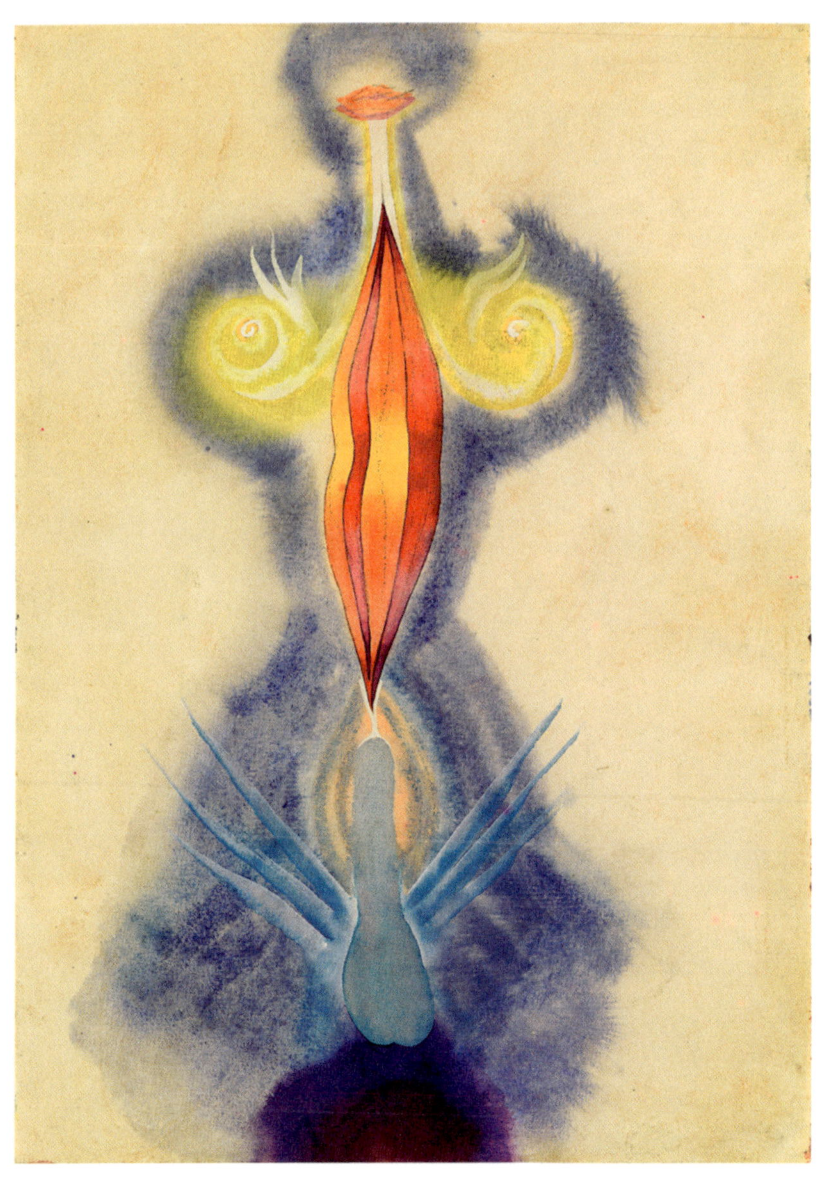

*Diagrams of Love: The
Androgyne II* 1940–1
Watercolour on paper
25.5 × 35

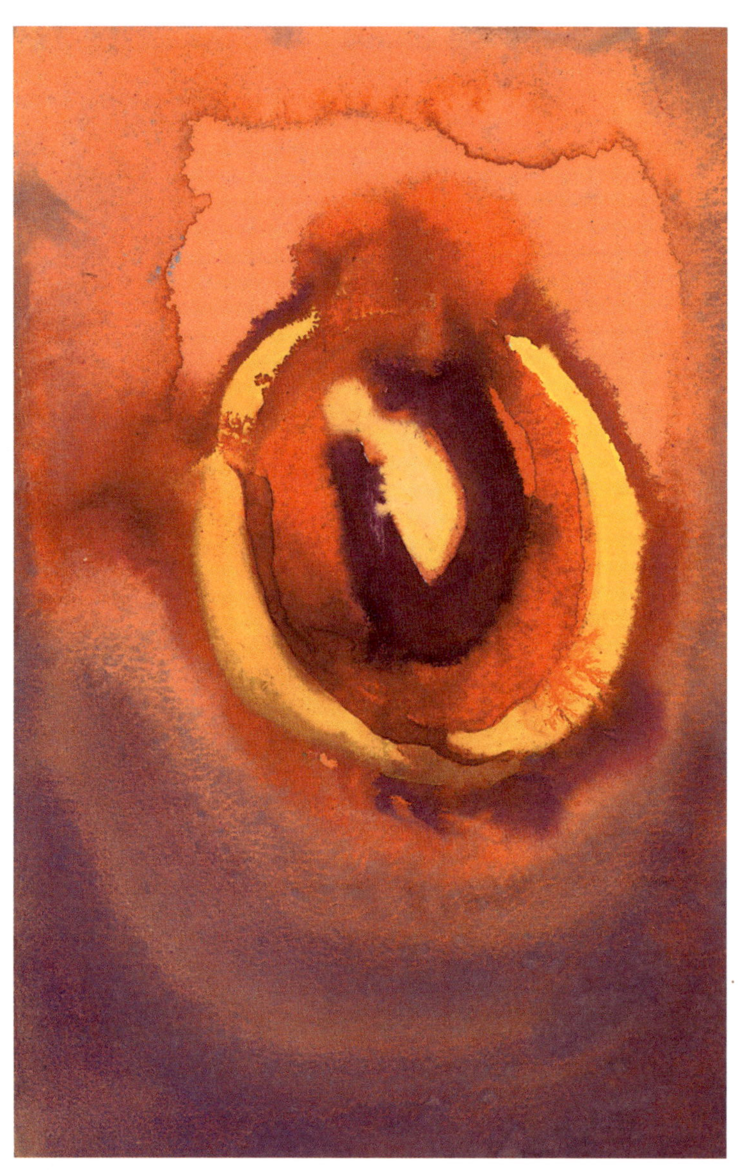

From the *Diagrams of Love*
series 1940, watercolour
on paper, 8.4 × 13

78

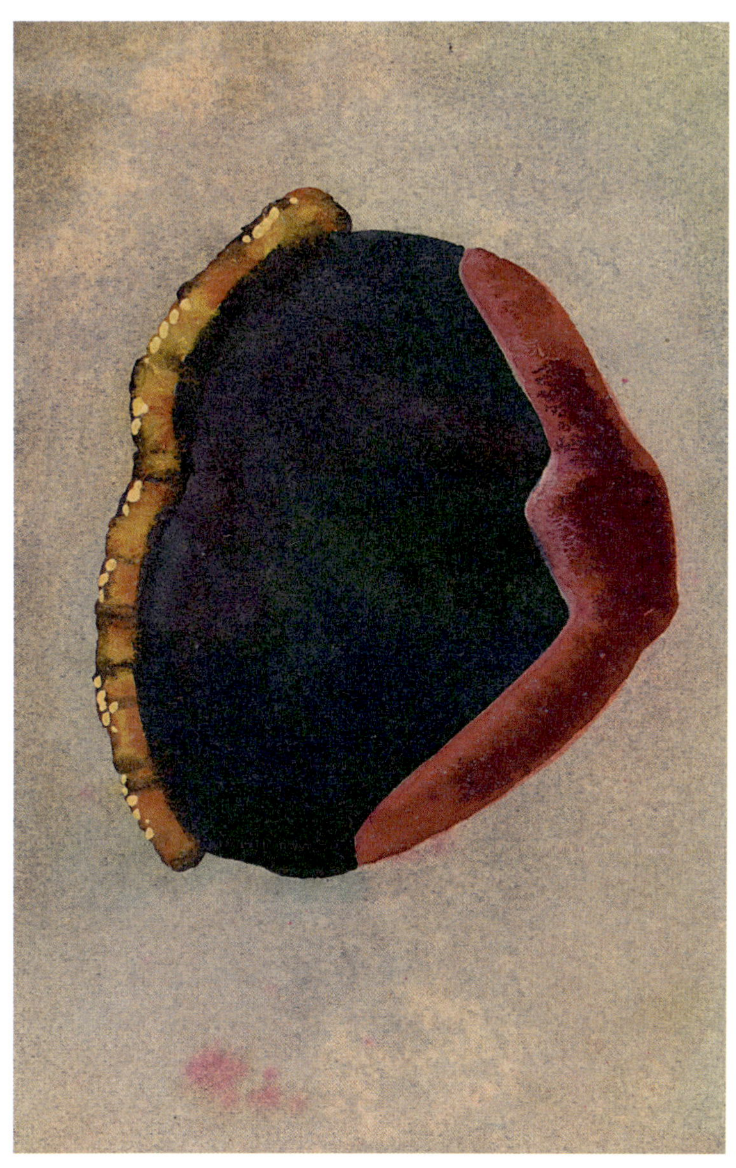

The Concealed Mouth
c.1940, watercolour on
paper, 25.8 × 16.3

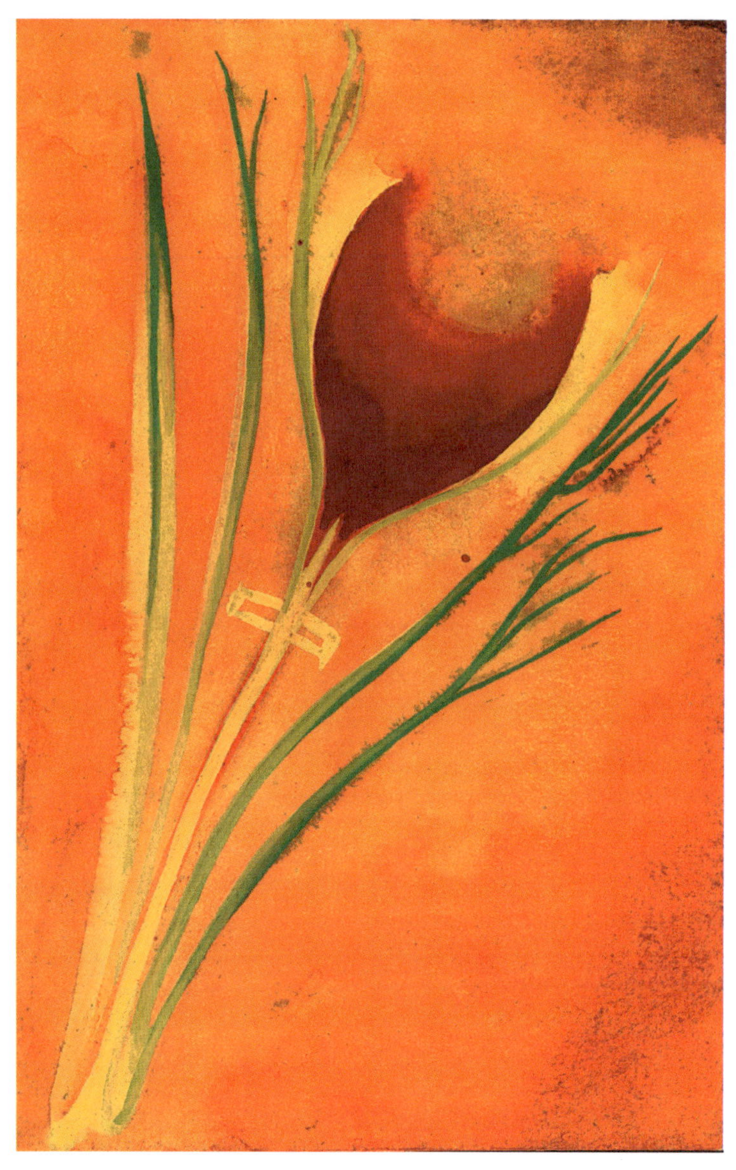

Heart of Corn 1940
Watercolour on paper
13 × 8.4

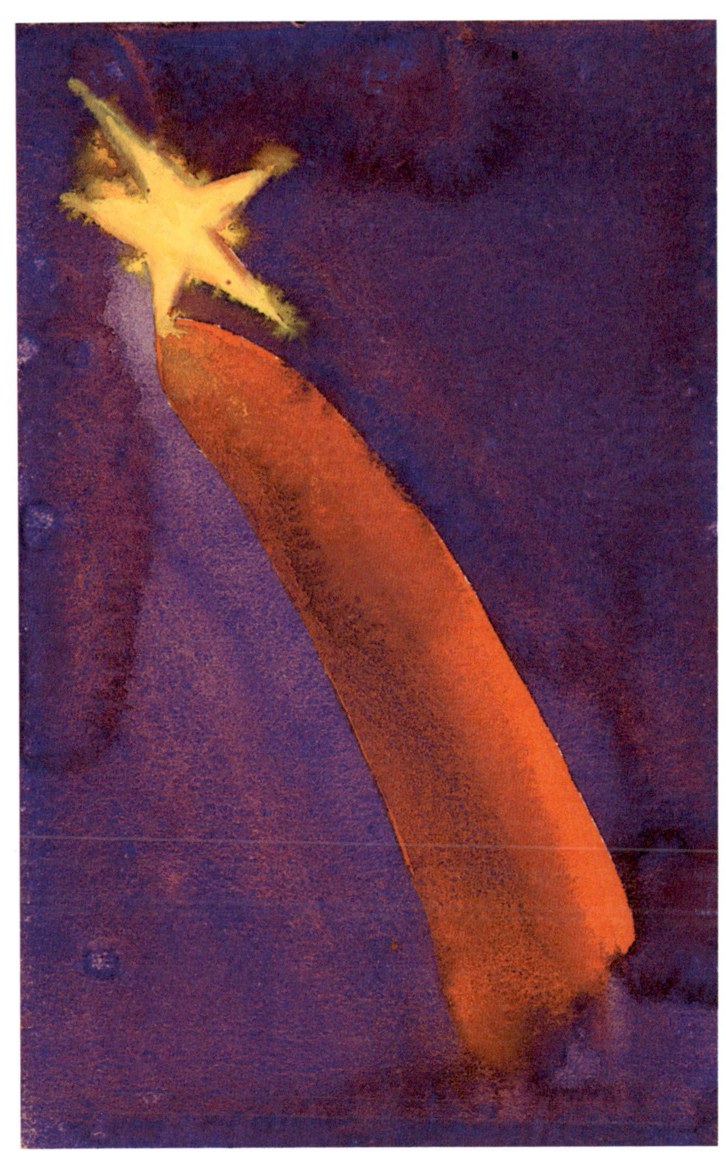

The Comet 1940
Watercolour on paper
13 × 20.3

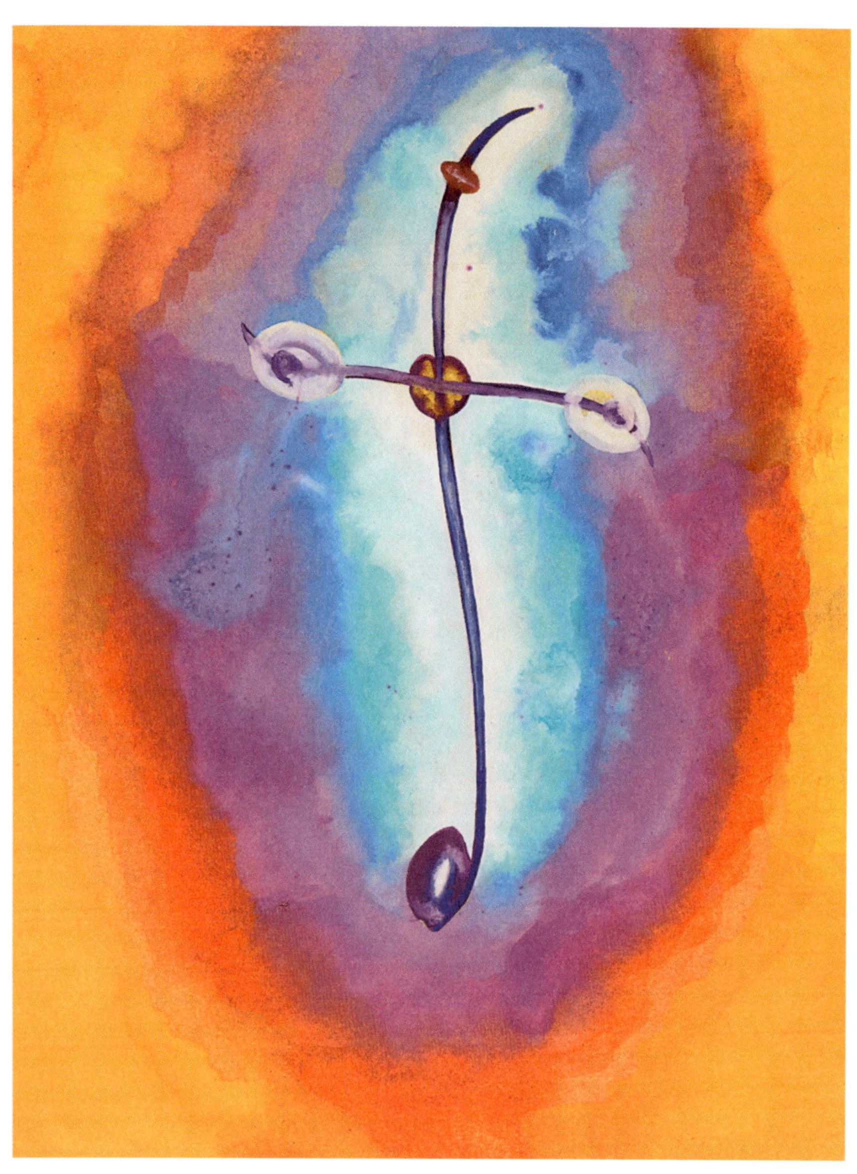

The Heart's Directions 1940
Watercolour on paper
13 × 18.2

82

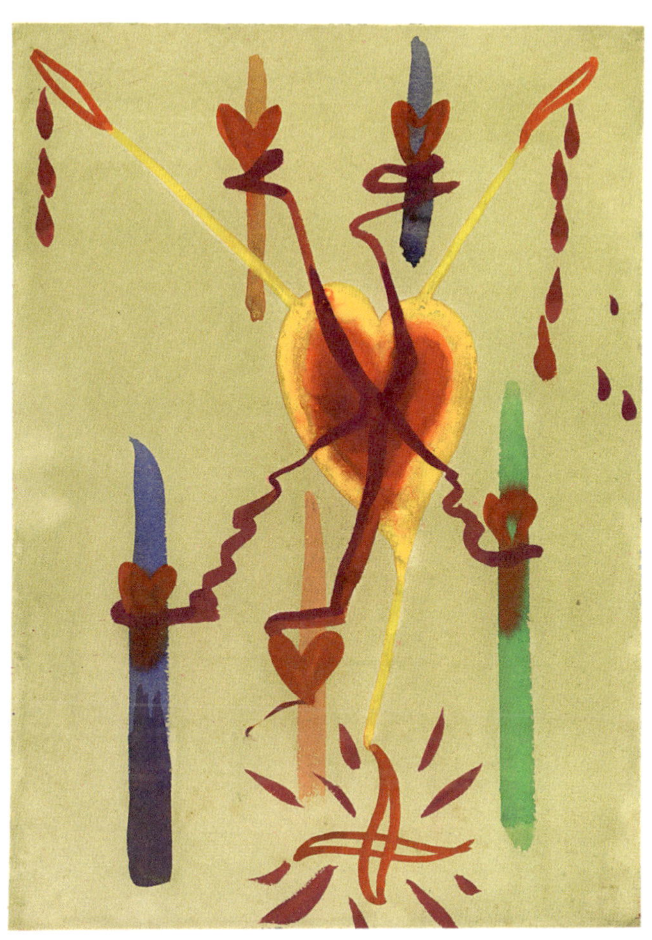

Circulation of the Blood
c.1941, watercolour on
paper, 35.5 × 25.5

83

Diagrams of Love II

It is as though
We were both dead
Not lifeless, free
From conditions

Our coats of skin
Cast aside
We meet in a mother-naked
Flame

He said in the shade
Yours is the breast of a dove

I knew that our love was deeper
Than all the qualities
And had existed
Before circumstance was

A leap a spark
Victorious metal's
Clang of triumph
Here acclaims his
Wished-for child

The wise say, Wipe out
Desire and ensue
The void of bliss

But what is content
If empty of you?

At your fingers' touch
The harp of my accord
Sounds its most vibrant string

Snow makes us aware
Of presences, but after
The thaw may something remain
Like snow in your garden
To take my footsteps' print

She saw his image in the clouds
In the sunset sky he saw her breasts

If he should pray
O three angel-weavers
Receive his words and make them garlands
Make flowery crowns as you are said to do.

Tears, a spray
Of the ocean

That which divides
Is all our link

Do not beg me
Never to leave you
When your love ceases
That day I go

The two moons coincide
What if my head pains me?
You in my heart
Make full moon always

How steps drag
Moving away from you
Hours lag
When you are not near

The springing step
That goes to meet you!
Moments that leap
Like an early breeze

I cannot enter by the door
That is unlocked at morning
I slip in at a side door
The chink that's wide at dusk
The narrow door between the ribs
That gives on the heart

Far from idyllic gleams or
The sun-warmed torso
I choke in the dark
And smother with regret for
That draught of well-being
Swallowed and still tasted
A constant air

O plasmic contact, ever to be renewed
Nothing can annul you
Nothing destroy

In phantasmagoric dark
Before sleep instead of folding
Into myself as I was taught to do
I plunge in another being
And touched by tendrils of forest
Or foam of ocean's tongue
At one with you then
I sink into the abyss.

So many messages
I look for but one.

I write letters
I write nonsense
He will not receive
The one letter I would send.

Are you covered?

Yes with linen
Satin fleece down
Still I shiver.
You also, or why do you ask?
You also are bare.

The skin is smooth
Between my breasts
The flesh whole
The bone unbroken

But the sternum's bland furrow
Hides a gash filled with flames

The Tree of Veins II 1940-1
Watercolour and gouache
on paper, 18 × 25.5

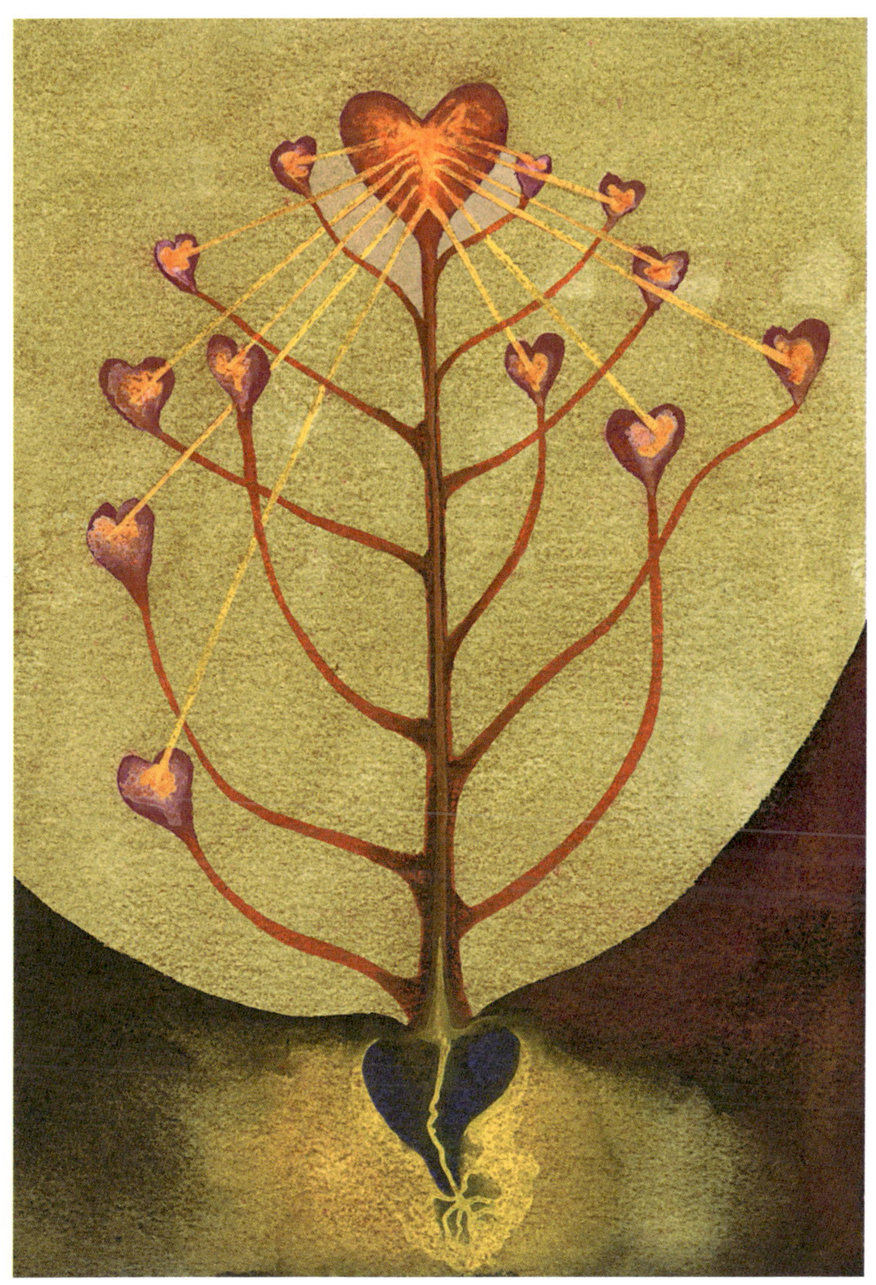

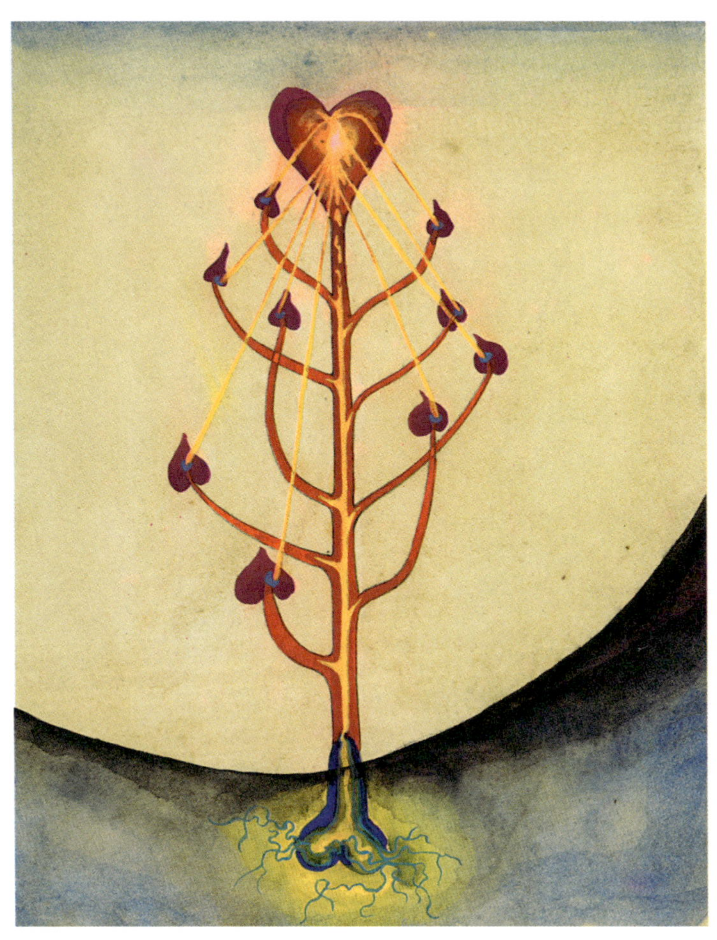

The Tree of Veins II c.1940s
Watercolour and gouache
on paper

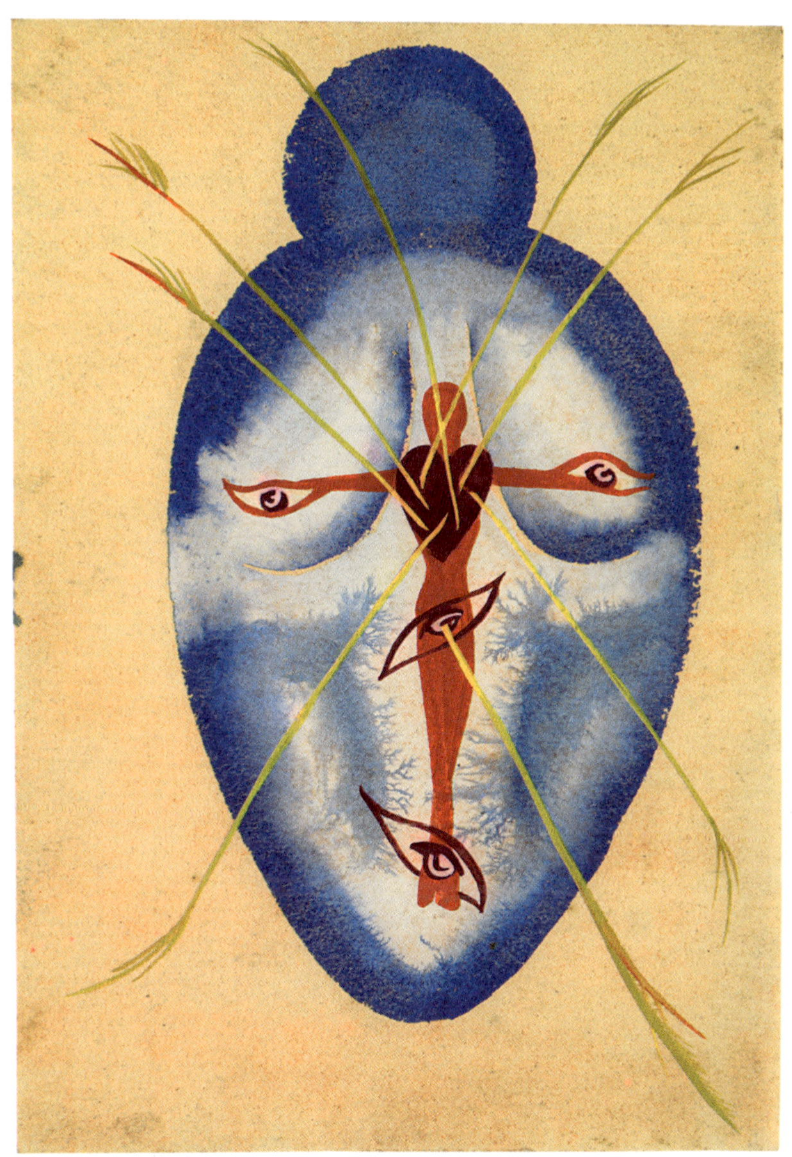

Diagrams of Love 1941
18 × 25·5

89

If I say that at 10 years old I imagined
Christ as a hermaphrodite I shall not
be believed. Yet it was so. Uncared for
by my distant parents, and needing
shelter, I fused the red hearted Jesus
with the blue cloaked Mary and made
a god with breasts. I did not know
the word El-Shaddai, nor any word to
express this image. I simply made the
image and worshipped it.

From 'Faith' an essay in the
unpublished autobiography
Until Twelve c.1949.

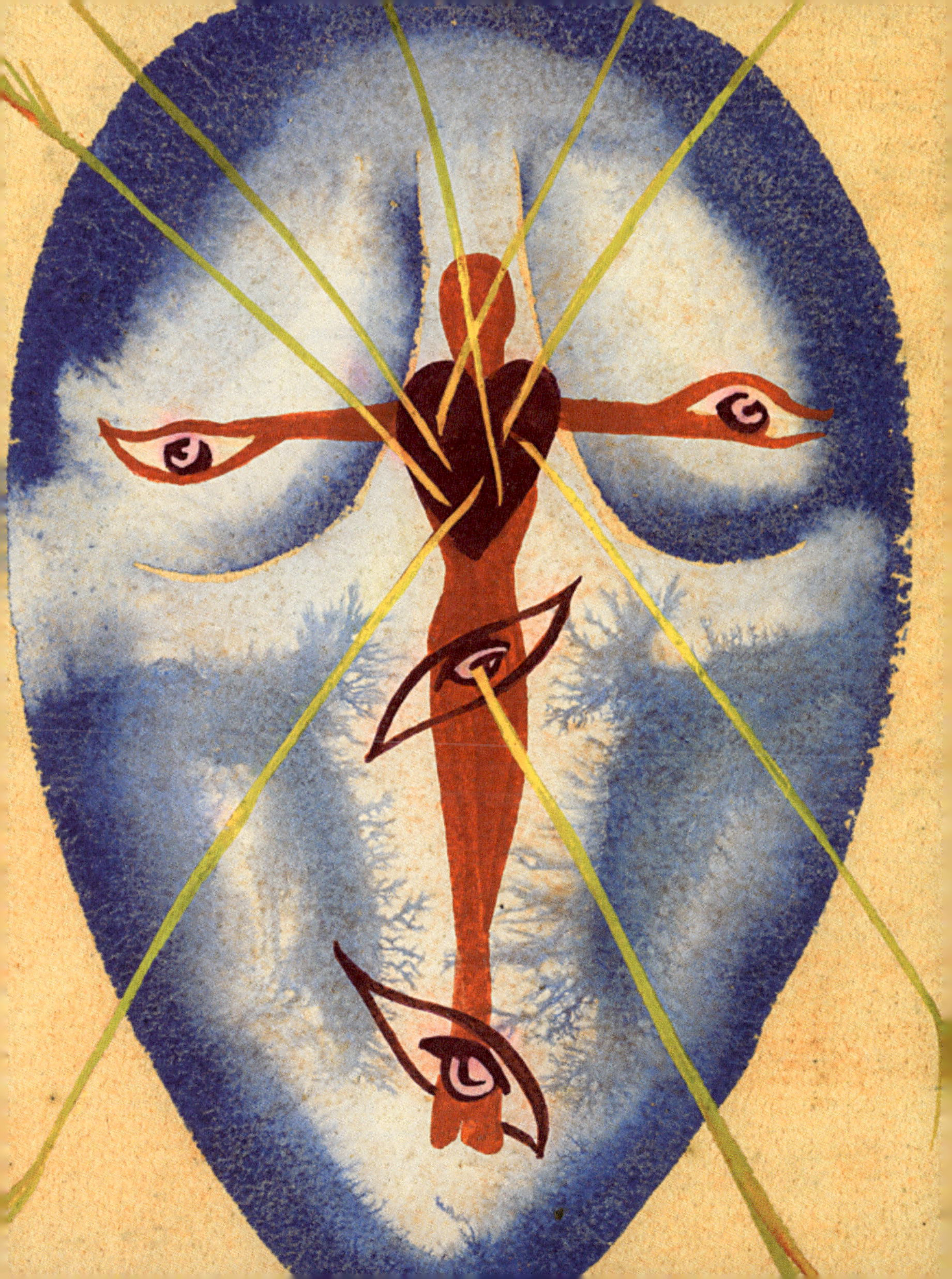

Notes

1

Hugh Urban, *Magia Sexualis: Sex, Magic, and Liberation in Modern Western Esotericism*, Berkeley, CA 2006, pp.7–8.

2

Phil Hine, *Queerying Occultures: Essays from Enfolding*, vol.1, London 2023, pp.x–xii.

3

Urban 2006, p.3.

4

For a general discussion of Evola's views on women see Paul Furlong, *Social and Political Thought of Julius Evola*, Oxford 2011, pp.121–3.

5

Maria De Naglowska, *Advanced Sex Magic: The Hanging Mystery Initiation*, trans. Donald Traxler, Rochester, VT, 2011, Kindle edition, pp.56–7.

6

See Marco Pasi, 'The Knight of Spermatophagy: Penetrating the Mysteries of Georges Le Clément de Saint-Marcq', in Wouter J. Hanegraaf and Jeffrey J. Kripal (eds.), *Hidden Intercourse: Eros and Sexuality in the History of Western Esotericism*, Leiden 2008, pp.369–400.

7

See Alex Owen, *The Place of Enchantment: British Occultism and the Culture of the Modern*, Chicago 2004, pp.35–6.

8

Paschal Beverly Randolph, *Eulis! The History of Love: Its Wondrous Magic, Chemistry, Rules, Laws, Moods, Modes and Rationale; Being the Third Revelation of Soul and Sex*, Toledo, OH 1874, p.151.

9

Ithell Colquhoun, 'Openings of the Body', *Quest*, no.4, 1970, pp.26-7.

10

The Ordo Templi Orientis is an influential Hermetic magical order dating from the late nineteenth-century Germany. Aleister Crowley became head of the order in 1925 and had a significant influence on the ritual and philosophical direction of the organisation.

11

Andre Breton, 'Prolegomena to a Third Surrealist Manifesto (or Not)' in *Andre Breton: Manifestoes of Surrealism*, trans. Richard Seaver and Helen R. Lane, Ann Arbor, MI 1969, pp.279–94.

12

Ithell Colquhoun, 'The Water-Stone of the Wise', in Alex Comfort and John Bayless (eds.), *New Road 1943: New Directions in European Art and Letters*, Billericay 1943, pp.198–9.

13

William Butler Yeats, 'Supernatural Poems' in Richard J. Finneran (ed.), *The Collected Poems of W.B. Yeats*, London 1991, pp.283–9.

14

For an earlier discussion of Colquhoun's wider interest in this theme see Victoria Ferintinou, 'The Iconography of Coniunctio Oppositorum: Visual and Verbal Dialogues in Ithell Colquhoun's Oeuvre', in Peter Forshaw (ed.), *Lux in Tenebris: The Visual and the Symbolic in Western Esotericism*, Leiden 2016, pp.363–96.

15

Kabbala Denudata: The Kabbalah Unveiled, trans. Samuel MacGregor Mathers, 1912 (1887), p.334, nos. 720, 723–4, https://sacred-texts.com/jud/tku/tku74.htm, last accessed 27 Sept. 2023.

16

From an undated personal note by Colquhoun in the Tate Archive. TGA 929/1/245.

17
Other drafts of this image were titled, *Heart of Corn*,
differing significantly from the image here on p.89.

18
See Theodor Reuss, *Parsifal and the Secret of the
Graal Unveiled*, 1920 (1914), https://www.parareligion.
ch/dplanet/html/parsifal.htm, accessed 27 Sept.
2023. See also Charles Stanfield Jones, *The
Chalice of Ecstasy: Being a Magical and Qabalistic
Interpretation of the Drama of Parzival*, Chicago 1923.

19
Jessie Weston, *From Ritual to Romance* (1920),
Global Grey ebook edition, 2019, p.62.

20
Rachel Rubenstein, 'What would Otherwise Remain
Unseen' in *Schema: World as Diagram*, exh. cat., The
Marlborough Gallery, New York 2023, pp.9–24.

21
Louisa Cook, *Geometrical Psychology, or The Science
of Representation: An Abstract of the Theories and
Diagrams of B.W. Betts*, London 1887, pp.12–17.

22
The Kabbalistic Tree of Life, originally derived
from Neoplatonically-inspired medieval Jewish
mysticism in medieval Spain, was later incorporated
into Renaissance esoteric Christianity and magic.
The visual representation of the Tree incorporates
ten spheres, or Sephiroth, which correspond to
various principles and are considered emanations
from God. In the nineteenth century, the Hermetic
Order of the Golden Dawn codified colour schemes
for the Tree over the four states of development,
ascending from the material to the spiritual; these
colour schemes are known as the King, Queen,
Prince and Princess scales.

23
KJV Exodus 28:4, 28:15–16.

Selected Reading

Andre Breton, 'Prolegomena to a Third Surrealist Manifesto (or Not)', in *Andre Breton: Manifestoes of Surrealism*, trans. Richard Seaver and Helen R. Lane, Ann Arbor, MI 1969, pp.279–94.

Ithell Colquhoun, 'The Water-stone of the Wise', in Alex Comfort and John Bayliss (eds.), *New Road 1943: New Directions in European Art and Letters*, Billericay 1943, pp.198–9.

Ithell Colquhoun, 'Openings of the Body', *Quest*, no.4, 1970, pp.9–10.

Ithell Colquhoun, *The Sword of Wisdom: MacGregor Mathers and the Golden Dawn*, New York 1975.

Louisa Cook, *Geometrical Psychology, or, The Science of Representation: An Abstract of the Theories and Diagrams of B. W. Betts*, London 1887.

Ida Craddock, *Heavenly Bridegrooms: An Unintentional Contribution to the Erotogenetic Interpretation of Religion*, New York 1918.

Maria De Naglowska, *Advanced Sex Magic: The Hanging Mystery Initiation*, trans. Donald Traxler, Rochester, VT 2011.

Victoria Ferintinou, 'The Iconography of Coniunctio Oppositorum: Visual and Verbal Dialogues in Ithell Colquhoun's Oeuvre', in Peter Forshaw (ed.) *Lux in Tenebris: The Visual and the Symbolic in Western Esotericism*, Leiden 2016, pp.363–96.

Richard J. Finneran, *The Collected Poems of W.B. Yeats*, London 1991, pp.283–9.

Dion Fortune, *The Esoteric Philosophy of Love and Marriage*, Newburyport, MA 2000.

Peter Forshaw (ed.), *Lux in Tenebris: The Visual and the Symbolic in Western Esotericism*, Leiden 2016.

Paul Furlong, *Social and Political Thought of Julius Evola*, Oxford 2011.

Edward Langford Garstin, *The Secret Fire: An Alchemical Study*, London 1932.

Wouter J. Hanegraaf and Jeffrey J. Kripal (eds.), *Hidden Intercourse: Eros and Sexuality in the History of Western Esotericism*, Leiden 2008.

Phil Hine, *Queerying Occultures: Essays from* Enfolding *Vol. 1*, London 2023.

S.L. MacGregor Mathers and Christian Knorr von Rosenroth, *The Kabbalah Unveiled: Containing the Following Books of the Zohar: The Book of Concealed Mystery; The Greater Holy Assembly; The Lesser Holy Assembly*, London 1962 (1887).

Alex Owen, *The Place of Enchantment: British Occultism and the Culture of the Modern*, Chicago, IL 2004.

Marco Pasi, 'The Knight of Spermatophagy: Penetrating the Mysteries of Georges Le Clément de Saint-Marcq', in Wouter J. Hanegraaf and Jeffrey J. Kripal (eds.), *Hidden Intercourse: Eros and Sexuality in the History of Western Esotericism*, Leiden 2008, pp.369–400.

Paschal Beverly Randolph, *Eulis! The History of Love: Its Wondrous Magic, Chemistry, Rules, Laws, Moods, Modes and Rationale; Being the Third Revelation of Soul and Sex*, Toledo, OH 1874.

Israel Regardie, *The Golden Dawn: The Original Account of the Teachings, Rites & Ceremonies of the Hermetic Order*, St. Paul, MN 1989 (1937).

Theodor Reuss, *Parsifal and the Secret of the Graal Unveiled*, 1920 (1914), https://www.parareligion.ch/dplanet/html/parsifal.htm (last accessed 27 Sept. 2023).

Charles Stanfield Jones, *The Chalice of Ecstasy: Being a Magical and Qabalistic Interpretation of the Drama of Parzival*, Chicago, IL 1923.

Alice Bunker Stockham, *Karezza: Ethics of Marriage*, Chicago, IL 1896.

Hugh Urban, *Magia Sexualis: Sex, Magic, and Liberation in Modern Western Esotericism*, Berkeley, CA 2006.

Jessie L. Weston, *From Ritual to Romance*, Cambridge 1920.

William Butler Yeats, *A Vision: An Explanation of Life Founded upon the Writings of Giraldus and upon certain Doctrines attributed to Kusta Ben Luka*, London 1925.

First published 2024 by order of the Tate Trustees by Tate Publishing,
a division of Tate Enterprises Ltd, Millbank, London SW1P 4RG
www.tate.org.uk/publishing

A catalogue record for this book is available from the British Library
ISBN 978 1 84976 880 1

Distributed in the United States and Canada by ABRAMS, New York
Library of Congress Control Number applied for

Design: Design Print Bind
Editor: Emilia Will
Production: Juliette Dupire
Introduction and selection of images and poems compliled by Amy Hale

Colour reproduction by DL
Printed and bound in Italy
Front cover: Ithell Colquhoun, *Diagrams of Love: The Bird or the Egg?* 1940–1
Measurements of artworks are given in centimetres, height before width

All images © Tate unless otherwise stated.
pp.9; 19; 28; 33–39; 41–3; 46; 50; 72–3; 75; 77–89 © Tate/Lucy Green
p.25 Image courtesy Unit London
p.29 (top right) Image courtesy Fulgur Press

Bequeathed by Ithell Colquhoun to the Tate Archive: pp.2; 61–3; 67; 75; 77; 87–91.
Part of the Ithell Colquhoun collection, Tate Archive. From the uncatalogued archive
recently transferred to Tate from the National Trust 2019: pp.5; 6; 9; 12; 15; 19; 22; 26–59;
64–6; 69–73; 78–83. Due to the nature of the acquisition, much of this body of work is
uncatalogued and details on the works not formally recorded. For more information
please contact Tate Archive.

Amy Hale would like to thank the following for assistance, contributions, comments,
interpretation and support in the preparation of this manuscript: Tony Fuller, Christina
Harrington, Phil Hine, Corella Hughes, Penny MacBeth, Katy Norris, Emma Sharples,
Richard Shillitoe, Maria Strutz, Georgia Van Raalte, and Marcus Williamson. I am
exceptionally grateful to Victoria Jenkins and the staff of the Tate Archives for tireless
assistance in obtaining images and documents. I am eternally grateful to Kate Tattersall
and Clive Boutle for their home and friendship. I am beyond grateful to Tate Publishing's
Emilia Will for realising this long-held dream and being a perfect editor. Thank you to
Design Print Bind for their beautiful book design. I am endlessly grateful to Rhett Aultman
and Robert Puckett for every manner of support they have provided to help bring this
book to the light of day.

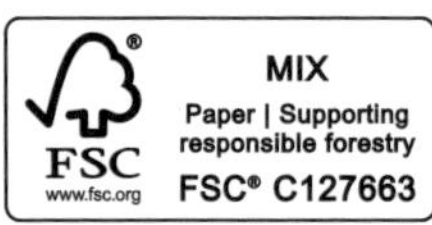